Prepare to be changed!

This book is not for the comfortable and complacent. What *Pilgrim's Progress* did for modern Christianity, *Saved Your Seat* now does for the post-modern church. It provides clarity of the Father's heart-intention for each of us in this journey of Grace and Love.

Through the candid telling of his story, Steve shares what it is like to have a promise from God only to watch it die and be resurrected by the Lord, beyond anything he could ask or imagine. Now he imparts the assurance that experiencing heaven is not something far off, but rather for every believer, right now.

This book is a welcome signpost to those who have always believed, "There's gotta be more than this..."

Diana T. Anderson
Chaplain and Worship Leader

A must read. *Saved Your Seat* takes you on a journey into the depths of God's love, acceptance and unwavering faithfulness. A refreshing reveal of the surety of our Divine purposes, promises and destiny.

Gino Lambano
Actor, Motivational Speaker and Life Coach

I have known Steve Dittmar for over twenty years. I have watched his journey with the Lord and have been amazed at the authentic love and power of Holy Spirit that he has embraced and displayed along the way.

I have known Steve Dittmar for over twenty years. I have watched his journey with the Lord and have been amazed at the authentic love and power of Holy Spirit that he has embraced and displayed along the way.

In his first book, *A River of His Forgiveness*, he took us to the deep places of the Father's love and mercy. This book proceeds to further move us into the brilliance of heaven and the glory of God.

Prepare to have guilt, shame or reproach fall off and be replaced with a resting in the security of bridal intimacy. The "devotional" style in which this book is written will aid the reader in strolling through its pages as Holy Spirit's presence emerges at each reading, to give His rich gifts of love and a wonderful re-clothing, from the inside out.

This book combines the best of experiencing the freedom of the Spirit, and the freedom of the Word, to bring this landmark work of God's nature and His ways, as He prepares us for an encounter that is more real than the world we live in... Freedom in the presence behind the veil.

Becky Ferris
Prayer Pastor
Director, Jubilee School of Ministry

This precious devotional draws us into the very heart of Our Father.

At a time when I felt I had failed Him in His service and had died to all visions, this testimonial (and being blessed to walk it out personally at Jubilee Church) lifted me into the perfect love of the Father.

I pray this teaching may fall like the rain, may these words drop down like dew, like showers on fresh grass and light rain on the turf, for it proclaims the way to Father's presence with Jesus and the Holy Spirit. Heaven on earth!

Thank you, Steve Dittmar.

Grateful for Sonship in Christ,
Marilyn Noorda
Friend

Steve Dittmar is a key contemporary influence that I feel challenged by and consider a truly original thinker of our time.

He is a "source" thinker, living from the truth that Jesus is the source of everything. Relieved to experience that nothing needs to be added to that truth, Steve invites us into a habit of living from victory's view.

Remember those tests where a card would be held up that looked like a blob and you had to state what the object was? Imagine you are sitting next to Jesus. A series of cards are held up: trouble, persecution, poverty and war. Black blobs of mess, despairing realities of earth.

Now, turn to see the response of Jesus. How does He see these realities? Can you hear His responses? Listen close. Yep, you will hear Him laughing. Once you get used to remaining in the company of Jesus, the problems on earth simply require a vision adjustment. Within each problem You will find there is not a single distress on earth that is unresolved in heaven.

The gift of this book is irrepressible confidence in Jesus. Consider those in the Bible and your own lives. What quenches joy, faith and hope? Mostly, our demands on time. Conforming victories to time can distract us in believing from the unseen.

There was a time when Abraham could not even imagine one child coming forth from him. Being a friend of God made Abraham's relationship with time very elastic; to the point that he not only could believe in one natural son but could see all the way out to Jesus coming from his family line and was overjoyed (John 8:56).

Is a victory valid only if you can see it in the natural world right now? Are you willing to be shown the victories that are generations away?

Welcome into the relief of sitting beside the One who can always see the end from any beginning.

Welcome into the relief of sitting beside the One who can always see the end from any beginning.

Lela Ruth Williams
Author / Songwriter

SAVED YOUR
SEAT

taking your place with Jesus in heaven

STEVE DITTMAR

ISBN: 148113678X
ISBN 13: 9781481136785

Library of Congress Control Number: 2012923168
CreateSpace Independent Publishing Platform
North Charleston, South Carolina

Jubilee Church, PO Box 777,
1169 Calle Suerte, Camarillo, CA 93012 | www.jubileechurch.org
Second Printing

CONTENTS

To every sojourner of His Presence,

you make God smile

and

to my children,

may the secret things revealed to me

be yours for eternity.

ACKNOWLEDGEMENTS

This book is the result of an amazing team effort.

I thank my writing team. Becky Ferris for taking the rough draft and praying it through, Lela Williams for focusing and forging me ahead, Diana Anderson for giving clarity and Eileen Chambers for her finishing craftsmanship.

I thank all of Jubilee Church.

Brian Rogers - you guarded the door and kept the ship moving. Rosie Bates - you encouraged others to stay in faith. Marilyn Noorda - your unwavering faith has made you great. Gino Gutridge - you never cease to amaze me how you get the message. Thank you Jubilee Warriors - your prayers, intercessions and giving of thanks carried me when I could no longer carry myself.

I thank my family. Nathan, Christy, Heidi, Jenna and David, my children, your love is genuine and an inspiration. Cammy, you are my beloved wife, fellow sojourner and friend. Thank you for journeying with me even during all the times I got us lost. You make the trip fun.

FOREWORD

I t is an unusual author who gives someone of no great name or renowned the honor of writing the foreword of his latest manuscript. However, those of us who know Steve Dittmar or, "Pastor Steve," as I have the privilege of calling him, this comes as no big surprise.

You see, Pastor Steve is a friend of God. He is someone who loves and is deeply loved by God. And they do things, *well,* His way.

As the story goes, five or six years ago, Pastor Steve and I were sitting in a gaudy Elvis Presley-themed hamburger joint geared for Americans on the outskirts of Jerusalem. A team of businessmen, artists and ministry leaders (me being one of them) was winding up a whirlwind trip to Israel and there, with Elvis crooning over our shoulders, Pastor Steve and I talked about, well, him writing a book.

Have you ever thought about writing a book, Pastor Steve? (*Translation: Pastor Steve, I think you need to write a book. Like yesterday.*)

He listened patiently and intently. With a pastoral-sort of smile. (*I'd rather to have a root canal, thanks very much.*)

O.K. Writing is not your forte. I get that. (*Who cares?! Pastor Steve, there are believers, who used to be like me, dying out there.*)

I suspected he knew that. Because, like Joshua, Pastor Steve has a call upon his life to bring God's children into their full inheritance and, believe me, the Lord knows how to speak to His leaders especially one like Pastor Steve.

(*Oh God. Let me part the Red Sea instead.*)

Well, *I* thought it was a good idea.

My perspective under the shadow of Elvis that day was that the Lord had gotten me to Pastor Steve's church in the nick of time. I had almost thirty years walking with Christ. I had prayed a lot, pursued a lot, believed big dreams, worked hard, did what I thought was God's will and made many life-altering, no-turning-back decisions. I went out on the limbs of faith, worshipped, prayed some more, gave, forgave, had notebooks worth of prophetic words, took the low seat and sold the farm.

The result? A barren life.

Instead of righteousness, peace and joy, I had stress, betrayal and brokenness. Nearing fifty, I was confused, disillusioned and ready to throw in the towel. Even worse, the irreversible decades spent pursuing God only mocked me. In the torturous, dark hours of night, I was pretty sure that I had screwed up my entire life. I ached inside. What ever happened to having "a hope and a future?" What did I do wrong here? All this work, where was the fruit? Did I miss some exit ramp somewhere?

Hey! I bought the field. Where the heck was the treasure?

I was shut down, in full cardiac arrest towards God, the One I loved. Broke my heart. And His. But He was not worried in the least. He sent me to Jubilee Church, a patchwork band of like-minded, out-of-the box, prophetic intercessory lovers of God that Pastor Steve and Cammy have shepherded for more than two decades. There, I found a pastor who understood the journey of those whom the Lord loves.

Now, to say that Pastor Steve is "a man of prayer," merely scratches the surface. He is someone who hangs out in a different realm. Honest, wise and able to laugh at himself, Pastor Steve loves God's word and is among most revelatory teachers I have ever heard. He is a Joshua, one well able to shoulder the call of bringing others into their inheritance.

O.K. I know I am biased. But it is still the truth.

Hang around Pastor Steve, hear him laughing with God in his office, see him weathering spiritual warfare or, better yet, dancing during worship and you will find that, as the old hymn so well states, "the things of this world grow strangely dim in the light of His glory and grace."

God encounters this man, Steve, a person who lives on earth out of the heavenly places in Christ Jesus. He has found the seat that Jesus has saved for him.

Me? I am alive again, a thankful lover more passionate and boastful of this God, the One who places His greatest promises in barren wombs.

And the great news? Pastor Steve got his book, *Saved Your Seat*, done. *Saved Your Seat* is an invitation to live beyond the veil with the One who loves you with an everlasting love. In short chapter format, it chronicles, in Pastor Steve's own way, his journey with

Christ and the revelations he has received about many aspects of God including promise, buying the field, surrender and the glorious life. The treasures buried here enable believers to experience the intimacy of a heavenly relationship now with God and to become the overcoming, victorious (and downright joyous) bride of Christ.

Trust me. If this book is in your hands, I suspect that God put it there.

Hungry? This is for you.

Disillusioned, confused and mad at God? No worries. Turn the page.

In a prison that looks an awful lot like Joseph's? Read on.

Want to be one with God, where He is, in the heavenly places? Oh yeah.

Eileen M. Chambers

Writer / Filmmaker

INTRODUCTION

This book, *Saved Your Seat*, is the fruit of a thirty-five year journey running into a sovereign event.

When I was nineteen, a surfer kid from Southern California, I accepted Jesus Christ as my Savior when a friend witnessed to me after a concert at my college. Since the moment I was born again, I have pursued the Lord, some thirty-five years now, much of that time being the senior pastor of a church in Camarillo, CA.

Then, in October 2011, I had an encounter with God in which I was caught up behind the veil into the presence of Christ, there to live and abide.

Wild. But wonderful.

Although I was still here on the earth physically—eating, sleeping, praying and working full-time at Jubilee Church—something so supernatural had taken hold of me. My entire point of reference changed. I was no longer living from an earthly place of dwelling but was literally seated with Christ in heavenly places.

Laughter. Joy. Peace. Righteousness. All the attributes of God literally flooded my being. I was overtaken. Overcome. Nothing else mattered in life. Although I knew that this was promised to all the Lord's redeemed, I was actually experiencing it!

For five months, I was not allowed by the Lord to speak of the encounter to anyone but my wife and a few close associates. Then He released me to teach others about what I was experiencing and to introduce them to the place where I had been dwelling. In the months that followed, the Lord encouraged me to write this book.

The genius of God is that He solidifies experience in quietness, testimony and recording. However, this book was written in the midst of much spiritual warfare and many personal trials that accompanied me as I wrote. Sometimes I would think, "God, if You hadn't commissioned me to write this, I would never have undertaken such a project."

But we both knew He had. Seven months later, I finished the manuscript.

Near the time of its completion, I experienced two visions exactly a week apart from each other. In the first, I saw myself in a little Cessna airplane taking off from a runway in Alaska. The scenery was rural and beautiful. Appearing before me as I lifted off the runway was a massive storm—dark, dangerous and menacing.

The storm was right in my path, standing between me and the mountain range I had to fly over. However, I knew this flight was important. I was headed to my wedding (I was the bride, so I understood this to be our heavenly wedding) but, seeing that threatening storm, I thought, "I need to land this plane and let the storm pass."

Immediately, I saw the Lord was sitting beside me. Then, as He spoke, He was inside of me. "Do not turn back," He said. "You are to fly through this storm. I will guide you. I will protect you. Stay in contact with headquarters and listen to the Holy Spirit."

With that, the vision ended.

For the next several days, I sought to understand how to fly into and through storms. Recalling that instrument-rated pilots are those who can fly without the benefit of natural sight, I asked the Lord what instruments we need in order to see in the dark. He showed me six instruments: praise, prayer, presence, promise, power and purity—which all keep us in perfect peace when practiced.

The next Sunday I entered into the second vision. I was in the same storm, being tossed to and fro, just as you might imagine in a little bitty plane. I would suddenly lose altitude and then get thrust skyward. Even though my plane was being bounced around, I kept practicing His presence and holding my faith.

As I did, from within me, a high-pressure system developed. Don't ask me how that works but weather buffs know that storms dissipate when high-pressure systems replace low-pressure systems in our atmosphere. As my high-pressure system grew, the sky turned blue around me. The turbulence stopped and I was flying in my own internal weather system—one that was coming from inside me!

What happened next was the strangest and most wonderful part of the vision.

Earlier in the week, I had wondered, "Why a Cessna?" I had seen myself years before flying fighter jets like the F16 but now my "vehicle" had been reduced to a Cessna!

Well, in the second vision, as the high-pressure system came out of me and the storm was displaced, the airplane began to break apart. This was not scary but liberating! It was fun. I was flying! The airplane, "the vehicle," was no longer necessary and I was flying through blue skies with my Lord to our wedding.

I believe these visions best describe both the warfare against our destinies and the means by which we will ultimately prevail as the accuser of the brethren is cast down and our identity in Christ is settled.

You and I have been called to a wedding. Nothing will prevent the Lord from our success, even though our outward man may be perishing (going from an F16 to a little Cessna), our inward man is being renewed daily. One day, we will fly and be with the Lord in the air.

I wrote *Saved Your Seat* very intentionally. I focused on creating short chapters to allow for pondering. In addition, I did not write out scriptures verbatim or reference them unless I felt that it was important to have the verse in the text. Finally, at the end of each chapter, I listed core scriptures (embodied in the text) for the purpose of further study or discovery and for those who may want additional substantiation.

I have memorized thousands of scriptures in my lifetime and find that telling the stories inside the scriptures opens us to new discoveries. My mind loves to categorize and file away information. In doing so, I have categorized and filed God neatly into my understanding but He doesn't live in a box.

What happened to me in October of 2011 was not a new experience but a continuation, a change of address. In writing this book, I felt it best to share what I experienced without trying to prove its truth with lots of sources. *Saved Your Seat* is a book of discovery, not a thesis on heaven or living in the Spirit.

My story is all in the Bible. I just didn't know that I could live there.

Jesus said, "The kingdom of heaven is like a treasure hidden in a field, which a man found and hid; and for joy over it he goes and sells all that he has and buys that field." (Matthew 13:44) This is my story of buying that field. It is for those who have set their hearts on pilgrimage, have left all to follow Christ or who have lost all in following Him.

The journey to our possession is precious in the sight of God and He is not ashamed to be called our God for He has prepared a city for us. What happened to me in October of 2011 is the content of this book. What happened to me in the journey of thirty-five years is its context.

The treasure you have found in Christ cannot be lost or stolen. It is reserved for you in heaven and is available to be enjoyed now. I hope those who have traveled long—as well as those just walking their first steps with Christ—will find help in these pages to see God and His wonderful works.

Core Scriptures:
Ephesians 2:6; Psalm 126:1, −2; John 14:17, 18; 2Corinthians 4:16;
1Thessalonians 4:17; Hebrews 11:16

1

IT'S GLORIOUS HERE!

I t's glorious here! The brilliance of heaven and the glory of God, in the face of Jesus Christ, now fill me. Laughter and joy are in the atmosphere; God's playfulness is ready to enjoy His redeemed. The ransomed of the Lord return, singing.

Peace, like a glassy sea surrounds the throne of grace; Father sits glowing in His love, acceptance, and joy. Christ, our high priest, stands, His compassion filling His face. Yes. I can pray—because He prays for me.

I approach the Father in childlike freedom. Running, I leap into His arms, which pull me up into His lap. "My, You are strong, glorious, victorious!" I exclaim as praise tumbles out of my spirit. I rehearse all the virtues and goodness of God that I can find.

I recollect scriptures and search for metaphors: "You are more beautiful than a summer day; kind and gentle, You are. You are merciful, gracious, and longsuffering; You abound in goodness and truth. You keep mercy to thousands." This is my favorite scripture that the Lord gave Moses in Exodus 34. I love saying this, lingering inside of every word, feeling the weight of glory and grace.

Soon I sense a cleansing of conscience, the sprinkling of blood, which purges away all residue of guilt, shame, or reproach. My accuser's accusations fade away. All I can hear is the assurance that my Beloved has accepted me. Words of life flow over my being as the washing of the water of the word cleanses my body.

I approach my Father again to proclaim boldly the confession of my hope, the promises made to me. Those promises are in the scriptures, visions, thoughts, feelings, words—all the impressions of heaven that have found their way into my life. In His presence, all has been transformed into my confession of hope. My hope, sure and steadfast has entered the presence behind the veil.

The expanse of these promises is massive. Each word has life inside. They are the very seeds of God, His nature, ways and workings. Experiencing these places in the Spirit, prepared for me in Christ, is more real than the world in which I live and work. The place of His dwelling—sitting with Christ, enjoying His fellowship and friendship—might sound quite presumptuous.

Indeed my experience was presumptuous, even privileged. My rational mind wondered, *How can this be?* My religious mind thought, *Blasphemy! Taking a place upon yourself you have neither earned nor can attain.* But there is a story of how this came to be. I wasn't always so free, and yet the seed of all that I have tried to describe (which is only a small part), was given in the very conception of my faith and imparted in every promise made to me by God.

You and I were made to be a dwelling place of God in the Spirit, a holy habitation of living stones built together to offer up spiritual sacrifices acceptable to God through Jesus Christ. It is a privilege to enter into the presence behind the veil and enjoy acceptance in Christ that permeates all my being—especially since I consider myself a "bruised, broken and breached man."

My efforts at righteousness left me this way. Of course I sinned but I was really trying to be righteous. The problem is that flesh and blood cannot inherit the kingdom of God nor does corruption inherit incorruption...but we shall all be changed. We are all being changed, from glory to glory. Even though it often seems more like from gory to gory, we *are* being changed.

You are much closer to change than you realize.

Core Scriptures:
Hebrews 10:19–23; Exodus 34:5–7; Hebrews 6:19–20; Ephesians 2:19–22;
1 Corinthians 15:50; 2 Corinthians 3:18

2

WE HAVE ALL BEEN HERE BEFORE

A holy hush invades the sanctuary; suddenly you are in the presence of God. Yet again, as you sit in your study reading or doing dishes in the kitchen, you sense the presence of the Lord wafting in, just as He would appear to Adam in the cool of the day.

This is the realm of the Spirit, which is ever-present, but not always present to us. This is where John was "in the Spirit" while on the island of Patmos, a political prisoner but not bound to the earthly realm. We may call these experiences "revelation" or "glory." We may call this "the Spirit" or "heaven."

Still, Heaven is a realm—both a place *and* an experience. Paul knew a man who went to Paradise and heard unutterable words. Now Paul wasn't sure if he had gone bodily or in the Spirit. John was in the Spirit when he went to heaven.

What happened to me in October 2011 is a mystery of sorts. My best explanation is that I had often visited the place that Jesus went to prepare for me but, in October of that year, I moved there. I took up residence inside the presence behind the veil. Sure, I still lived on earth but my dwelling had changed; meaning where I live *from* had changed. I began to abide with the sovereign Lord, seated with Christ in heavenly places.

How cool was that? Believe me. I am not speaking euphemistically. I am talking about a real place.

For five months I could share with no one the wonderful discoveries I was finding in His presence behind the veil. The Lord's instructions were very specific: "Do not tell anyone about what is happening. Just learn to live and minister from here." What the Lord said next made me chuckle. "I don't care what you speak about." Jesus was training me to live in the place prepared for all of us in Christ and *learning to minister* from my place in Christ was more important than what I said.

I did what I was told. I enjoyed His presence and celebrated this new home in heaven, in the Spirit. The Lord was gracious, taking me on tours of this wonderful place now my home. I saw the word of God living—really living. I could even go inside His word and experience it. I experienced the reality that the joy and pleasure of heaven are uninterrupted by the affairs of this earth.

Heaven is only aware of what Jesus has done. As far as heaven is concerned, it is finished.

Salvation belongs to our God and to the Lamb. Laughter fills the air and there is great expectancy but, inside, even greater patience.

Yes. I was learning through prolonged exposure what the rule of heaven looked like from heaven's perspective. I was not surprised or caught off guard by most of what I experiencing during those first five months, but rather the word was coming alive in me.

You see, in the realm of heaven, there is such confidence and awe at the finished work of Christ. I know I believed that, but now I really *believed* - or should I say, I experienced the hope that enters behind the veil.

My years of striving now just seemed foolish. Even though it is not foolish to want to see God's Kingdom established on earth, how I was going about trying to create that change was foolish. I would see in the Spirit, then go rushing to bring what I had seen into the earth. Unable to succeed, I would grow frustrated. This frustration, coupled with the urgency that rises from the earth and her woes, destroyed my confidence, leaving me harried and frazzled.

The encounters I had with God in October 2011 brought a renewal to my life and ministry. Now I am learning to rule from here in the fruit of the Spirit and the grace of our Lord Jesus Christ. I am constantly amazed at the confidence, patience, love, and longsuffering of Jesus.

Again, I had known this but now I *knew* it.

Core Scriptures:
Revelation 1:9–12; 2 Corinthians 12:1–5; Revelation 4:1–3; 3:21; 5

3

WHY CAN'T I TAKE IT HOME WITH ME?

In His presence is the fullness of joy!

It's true; the Lord is joyful, playful in His affections toward us. In His presence, I am unaware of my tribulations and even petitions. I may come to Him laden down with my struggles and troubles but in His presence they fade away. I am only aware of Him and myself. In heaven, I am the object of His affection, love and joy.

I may be a little boy playing with His Father or a young man listening to His instructions. Still, what I enjoy most is being myself in the moment of eternity. I see God's promises to me growing in depth and worth. Even though I have failed to claim the fruits of some of these promises, they are there, eternal, living and alive in Christ. They are not gone, diminished or fading away. They are eternal in heaven, reserved for me.

I have always enjoyed the presence of God. Now I enjoy it much more.

When I was young, I would worship, pray, witness, work, and love— I did many things. My only ambition was the manifestation of His kingdom and His word in the earth. What I didn't know was that I had access to enjoy and abide in His kingdom apart from this world.

So, I would become undone in His presence and awakened into new realms of His glory. I would write down what I heard and saw, then try to replicate it on earth.

Doing this brought me both success and heartache. His presence was the fulfillment of joy and there were pleasures forevermore at His right hand. God invades our world and offers such joy and pleasure in our prayer and worship of Him. However, what I learned (the heartache) was that I could not just rush away and replicate what I had experienced with Him.

In His presence abides the hope of our confession, a beautiful dwelling place given to us by the Spirit through Jesus Christ, the living word. When I go and sit, I enter into His rest, ceasing from my striving. There, I watch my Lord. There He is, sitting on the throne of grace—regal, joyful, full of mercy and grace. Jesus Christ, appearing in the presence of God beckons me to come. "Stay a while. Look around. Seek those things above where I am seated at the right hand of God."

In the presence of God, Jesus Christ has accomplished it all. Everything is finished. There is nothing to be added nor can anything be subtracted from His great work. Sure. Here on earth, it is a very different story. The tide comes in and goes out. Storms come and go. That is just the way it is here on earth. It is temporary.

However, heaven is eternal. It is filled with redemption, victory, overcoming and rejoicing. There I dance, sing, and sit—not in my victories but in the Lamb's victory! That is the way it is seated in Christ, and try as I may to bring this to earth, I cannot, not on my volition. Attempting to do so, I am merely like Jack and the Beanstalk climbing up and trying to steal the giant's hen that lays the golden eggs.

It just is not right to use God as the means to fulfill some purpose. He delights in being enjoyed. In His presence, I have complete access to everything plus the authority of sonship. I can rule but am not free to do as I want with what I am given—because everything goes back into worship and fellowship.

I have always been a glory seeker, not of man's but of God's glory. I did not seek glory for myself but rather to handle and share. I have seen much and have learned that revelation is like looking through a window. Transformation is what happens *after* that revelation of Christ crucifies you.

Living behind the veil with Christ starts with a window we see through, then a door we walk through. It is a promise that grows into a pursuit (then maybe even a prison). In the end, it is Jesus and you. You and the Father. You are one greatly loved, highly favored and bringing much pleasure to Him.

Nothing else is needed. All has been given. All is yours and you are His.

Core Scriptures:
Psalm 16:11; 1 Peter 1:3–5; Hebrews 4:10; 14:16; 9:23–28

4

THE SEED OF GOD

The nature of God is given through promise. First, the Lord reveals Himself to you.

In 1976, the Lord revealed Himself to me. I learned that He was the Christ, the Son of the living God. I accepted Jesus into my heart and that seed of faith—the promise I would be saved if I believed He died for my sins and was raised from the dead for my justification, confessing Him as Lord—was the seed of my new birth.

Immediately I was snatched out of the fire, changed from a lost boy to a found son. I *knew* I was saved. Though I still had many demons to resist, I had seen the Lord and had no doubt that He had saved me.

Words, promises and the scriptures suddenly became alive to me. I read the Bible voraciously. I was, I am sure, in the ICU of heaven being fed intravenously. I was so hungry. Nineteen years of separation and sin had left me famished to know God. Jesus Christ was the way of truth and life, and I knew there was no other way to the Father.

Soon, I was filled with the Holy Spirit which further immersed me in the word. I memorized scriptures and served in a local ministry. In every way, the Lord was establishing my boundaries, surrounding me with new favor and setting me apart for a lifetime of service. Within four years, I was married, a new father and youth pastor. In 1984, my beautiful wife, Cammy, and I started Jubilee Church, where we are still pastoring some five children and one grandchild later.

However, despite the favor from heaven, zeal for God and the promises that were growing, I was still aware of my fears. I sought comfort in biblical characters, following their lives in scripture, living in their stories and trying to find truths while avoiding their pitfalls.

As I grew in my place in the Lord, I was learning that promises are like seeds scattered everywhere in the scripture. You read a story and a promise begins to unfold. It is not like a voice comes down from heaven and says, "This is yours." You just feel a nod like "Go ahead. Believe." or "This is for you." Even the feeling, "I would give anything to experience that."

The invitation to believe, the go-ahead to take it, coupled with the internal desire to experience are all part of the voice of God awakened in you by the Holy Spirit.

Taking is faith and faith is pleasing to God. With the taking often comes a sense of satisfaction, well-being and liftoff. You can almost hear heaven say, "Congratulations, you have just conceived. His seed has been born in you!" Over the years that seed will take hold of your being until His nature has become yours and His promises are your dwelling place.

According to the Bible, the seed of God is eternal and incorruptible. It will yield a crop in our hearts if we hold it until maturity. However, in the meantime, it just might kill you.

It is a glorious thing to hear God's voice. All of His children do, for scripture says, "for as many as are led by the Spirit of God, these are sons of God." (Romans 8:14) Jesus said, "My sheep hear My voice and I know them, and they follow Me." (John 10:27) You see, everything in the kingdom is received by faith, conceived by faith and kept by patience. The word spoken has to be received, then kept patiently in secret in His presence.

Core Scriptures:
Romans 10:9–10; Acts 2:38–39; 2 Peter 1:4; Luke 8:11–15;
Hebrews 6:11–12

.

5

KNOWING GOD

Jesus shared openly about the life He had to give—specifically that He had authority to give eternal life to as many as the Father had given Him.

In our dead state (the state we are in before we hear the Son of God's voice), we are living in and of this world instead of being in God's world. When we hear His voice, faith comes and we live and can see the kingdom of God. Pursuing the Lord in His presence, and valuing His voice in His word, results in a wonderful relationship. He knows us and we know him.

I can still remember the night that I got saved. I was nineteen years old, a California surfer wanting to be a rock star. After an Andre Crouch concert, a young girl asked me, "Do you know the Lord?" I said, "I am trying to." Her blunt reply startled and provoked me. "Well, then you don't."

She was right. Either you know the Lord or you don't.

There has to be an introduction coupled with the recognition that Jesus is the Son of God—not simply a prophet or great teacher—but *the* Son of God, who gave His life as a ransom for many. When you hear the voice of the Son of God, then you will live. You are born again. You can see and enter the kingdom of God.

It is your first step as a child of God, this introduction to Jesus as Savior and Lord. Through faith we agree and confess that "Jesus is my Lord"—which Jesus defines as eternal life. "And this is eternal life, that they may know You, the only true God, and Jesus Christ whom You sent." (John 17:3)

I have never forgotten the night that young girl asked me that direct question, "Do you know the Lord?" or when Larry Mathews, the man who had invited me to the concert, explained to me (and Gerald Davis, a drummer in the band I was in) what it meant to accept Christ. As we stood outside of the Ventura College Gymnasium, Larry said that Jesus came to earth, that He had died for our sins and was the only way to know God.

I listened intently, concentrating on his every word. Everything inside me did not want this moment to pass me by. I blurted out, "Can we pray right now?" which really shocked Larry. "Of course," he replied.

We joined hands, bowed our heads and prayed: "Jesus, I believe You are the Son of God and died for my sins. I believe that You rose from the dead. I ask You to come into my heart, forgive my sins and make me the man I cannot make myself."

Immediately, something happened inside me. Somehow, I knew that I knew God.

Going home that night to my parents' house, I was light as day. I was born again. I did not know yet what that meant but that was what they told me had happened. Jesus was in my heart. Me! A guy who had never stepped one foot into a church. Happy as I was, I went outside and smoked a joint to celebrate (because that was what I did when I was happy). Nothing odd happened. There were no thunderbolts or condemnation from heaven. I just went to bed, happy.

When I got up the next day, I asked my mom if I could borrow her Bible. Right there, I read the entire book of Matthew. For the next week, I read my homework assignments and the Bible until I put the school books down and read only the Bible. I was discovering that the Spirit of God was my teacher and sanctifier.

A week later, as my friends and I were getting high, I tried to share everything that had happened and what I was learning. I found that I could not communicate the Lord I was coming to know. I was confused and my friends ridiculed me.

Then and there, I decided that pot was no longer for me because it clouded my ability to see and speak. I stopped smoking without anyone telling me. It was, instead, the Holy Spirit showing me.

My clarity in Jesus grew daily as I sought Him, read His word and prayed. Two weeks after I was saved, I went to my first church service. There, in the front row with my mother and father, I sang songs I had never heard before but now so enjoyed.

After service, I grabbed the phone book, searched the yellow pages and found another church that I could go to that same morning. Hours later, I went back to the same church for its evening service. I was a new baby and like all infants, I wanted to eat.

Core Scriptures:
John 17:2–3; 5:25; 3:3; 14:26; 2 Thessalonians 2:13

6

FOUR THINGS TO DO

A t the end of the Sunday evening service, a man introduced himself and then asked me about myself. My appearance, including long hair, made it obvious that I was new to the church and it must have been clear that I still had many issues for the Spirit of the Lord to address. When he heard I was new, he offered me this simple advice (which I have shared many times since that day).

"There are four things you can do to grow in your relationship with Jesus," he said. "Pray. Read His word. Fellowship in His church and tell others what Jesus has done for you." This was the best advice I could have received. Talk to God. Read His word. Be with His people and tell others (witness) about Jesus.

It was simple. I could easily do these things. So I prayed and read. I shared my experience with others and began to be a part of that church—the People's Church in Ventura, California.

It's funny. Almost forty years later, I am still doing these four basic things, especially prayer. I often pray, spending time with my Father (something we used to call "devotional time, alone time or quiet time") and this simple discipline has opened the door of discovery to all that I know today.

Daily, I sit with Jesus, listening to His voice in His word, praying, sharing my heart, praising and thanking Him with the word of God being such a part of this alone time. (When I bought my first Bible, thankfully someone told me to mark it up any time I sensed the Lord speaking and I still do underline or highlight verses, many Bibles later.)

Living in the body of Christ, being in church and being known by others, makes all the difference. The walk we live in is filled with distraction, disappointment, and destruction. We need each other and need to be provoked to love and good works. We are selfish in the flesh. It is so easy to become offended by someone in the church, to be hurt or bored because we neglect our time and drift away. Our gatherings each Sunday, and through the week, are miniature exercises in rapture. The word "church" means "called out." The word, "assemble" means "to collect." So we are the "called out ones, collected together." The word "assemble" also means "gather together" in reference to the rapture of the church.

In this light, we gather together and exhort one another more and more as we see the day of the Lord approaching. "Exhort" means "to call close," as in a huddle. Putting all the pieces together, we have been called out of the world and collected together. We call one another close and communicate Christ to each other.

Witnessing or telling others what the Lord has done was easy at first. He was doing so much in my life. Many people noticed a dramatic change and a radical reversal of direction. They naturally asked what had happened and I told them, "Jesus saved me."

I witnessed to His work in me, inviting everyone to be saved. Many were. But, from the initial combustion, things will run their course. Six to nine months after I got saved, my flesh caught up with me. I had been propelled into a new life and thought the emotion of it would never fade but it did. I soon found that I was still the same person in many ways.

But it was too late.

I had burned my bridges by witnessing to my friends. I had entered into a new community (the body of Christ). I had encountered God in prayer and His word. I moved forward in those moments.

After making the decision to love and serve Him, I found I was stuck. (Thank God I was stuck!) I had bumper stickers all over my car which read, "I have decided to follow Jesus," "I found it," and "You'd smile too if you were going to heaven."

The problem was that I wasn't smiling anymore.

Core Scriptures:
Luke 11:1–4; Philippians 4:6–7; John 8:31–32; 17:15–17; Acts 2:42;
Hebrews 10:24–5; Mark 5:19–20; Acts 1:8; 2 Thessalonians 2:1;
Matthew 24:31

7

OUT IN THE SNOW

God's ways are pure genius. He has a way of so enthralling you. Then, when you are free of self and fear, He shows you His promises. Gazing at the vista of your inheritance into your future, you say, "Yes. I will give anything to have that." And you sell the farm to buy the field and to gain the treasure you found. Still, the field belongs to God. You may purchase more than what you bargained for.

In my intoxication of new birth, I had prayed, "Father, I want the world to be different because I have followed You. I want to change the world." I heard the Father say, "You will change the world but first I have to change you." I thought, *That's cool. I am going to change the world.*

There it was: my first promise. Oh how I seriously underestimated the cost of changing me. I thought, *How long could that take?* Yet, not even a year into my salvation, I was already backsliding. I was still following my new ways (remember, I was stuck, trapped) but in my heart I felt discouraged and wanted to quit. Proverbs says, "A backslider will be filled with his own ways, but a good man is satisfied from above." I was full again of myself, no longer satisfied from above.

But I had committed to travel as part of a ministry team to Sun Valley/Ketchum, Idaho. The day after Thanksgiving three other young disciples and I left California with our ministry leader to start a "youth ministry." Sullen and sorry for myself, I drove those seventeen hundred miles from home, arriving to find that we were somewhat unexpected.

The Episcopal church we were coming to work with had a nice condo for Joann (the one girl on our team) but only temporary housing, for the guys until we found work, a small cabin on the outskirts of the National Forest. This cabin had electricity and water but no heat. When we put our things inside the cabin, the snow stayed on the carpet, long after we had stomped if off!

As we went out to the snow-covered road to say good-bye to our team leader, Tom Brock, and the motor home disappeared in the dark, I had the most frightening and wonderful discovery. "I am backslidden," I said to myself. "I can't find God. How am I ever going to survive this?"

My wake-up call occurred on a snow-covered road in Ketchum/Sun Valley Idaho! The Lord had gotten my attention. I was standing in the snow without the ability to get a hold of God. My fire had burned dim and my oil was almost out. Like the foolish virgins in the Bible, I had neglected to fill my oil when it had run low. Now I would have to go and buy oil.

I started praying again with fervor. The three of us guys got jobs, moved into a studio apartment and worked with the local churches. I even got to ski. But, what I remember the most that first winter was not any of the miracles of provision or fruits of ministry. I remember my long walks at night on the snow-covered roads, crying out to God that my cold heart would come alive again.

Desperation and desire move us toward God and I was desperate. Just as I had done the night I got saved, I sought the Lord, "Please don't pass me by. Help me, Jesus." Despite the circumstances in Ketchum being very favorable and the fact that we were successful in our ministry, my heart ached for the Lord.

I was buying the field, one prayer at a time, one late-night walk at a time, one movement of my heart toward the Lord. I was buying the field that contained the treasure. I had come to know God again.

Core Scriptures:
Acts 2:1–15; Matthew 13:44; Proverbs 14:14; Jeremiah 29:13; James 4:8;
Luke 18:35–43

8

BUYING THE FIELD

W hen we encounter the Lord by His Spirit and within His word, we discover treasures that are worth everything we have (and very often require everything we have) in order to buy the field containing the treasure.

Let me be honest. I used to wonder at the wisdom of the parable of the hidden treasure. According to the parable: "Again, the kingdom of heaven is like treasure hidden in a field, which a man found and hid; and for joy over it he goes and sells all that he has and buys the field." (Matthew 13:44) *Why didn't he just grab the treasure and run?* I would think. Answer? Because he couldn't do it anymore than I could take the treasures I have discovered in heaven, in the Spirit, in His word and then run. We have to buy the field and the field costs us everything we have.

Think of God's treasures as His mineral rights.

In most parts of the world today, you can own land but not necessarily own the mineral rights. Take for example my house. It was built in a tract and although I have the right to live on top of the land, I have no right to anything beneath ground-level (except to plant a tree, put in sprinklers or maybe a pool). If, as I planted my tree, I discovered gold, oil, silver or any other mineral (including water) none of them would be mine because I don't own the mineral rights to the property.

When we discover spiritual gold, we have to purchase the mineral rights, which is basically done like this: "Wow! I have never seen this before. This is the best promise I have ever heard." You say the promise, underline the Bible, write it down and memorize it. You do all the important things necessary to secure the location of this treasure.

Joy floods your soul and you see something of such incredible worth that you are willing to give anything to have the mineral rights. It is an exchange with God but, since He does not believe in mortgaging, He promises that the field will be ours, while requiring that patience perfect its work in us.

After being saved, the transfer of title began in my life. In Sun Valley/Ketchum, Idaho, I discovered for myself the treasure of knowing God in a face-to-face relationship beyond my initial salvation. Discovering this treasure, I began to make inquiries, "How can I own this?" I learned that I would have to buy the field. "I will, no matter what it costs me. Knowing God face-to-face is worth everything," I said.

Of course, I was not aware of what it would cost me, anymore than a young man or woman can know what it will cost them to have a relationship of love and trust within their marriage. They see the treasure but, to buy the field comes at a cost of a lifetime of commitment. In essence, the field, where the treasure is, will take a lifetime to purchase.

Of course, the promises of God are all fulfilled in Jesus and are in Him, the Yes and Amen, given to us by grace, not of works that we can boast of earning them. That is why healing, deliverance and the Baptism of the Holy Spirit are given freely and are available immediately.

But some promises are attached to buying the field. They are lifetime promises, treasures that we see a far off and journey towards. We bury the treasure where we found it (that moment of revelation and experience). We mark the place and, then, go and make inquiries, intent on buying the land where the treasure we have found is buried.

For me, God's words came back as I entered into escrow. I bought the field where intimacy with God was buried, knowing that I would have to give my life to prayer. I was doing that already but the instructions I received became clearer as I went on.

Like me, you will need to enter into honest face-to-face exchanges with God and allow His coming to affect your going. You will lose your life to entertain His. You will have to seek Him with all your heart and, when you find Him, yield again to His coming.

Core Scriptures:
Matthew 13:44; Psalm 27:8; 2 Corinthians 1:20; Ephesians 2:8–9;
1 Corinthians 13:12; 2 Corinthians 3:18

9

I LOST THE TREASURE

As time went on, I continued to make payments on my land. I practiced every form of prayer and found His presence. I gleaned, yielded and learned His ways. I didn't do what I was doing simply to gain the land but, rather, so that I could learn the ways of the land. I studied the culture of the King: His ways and His likes.

I would exercise my spirit in prayer or praise, learning something new about the face of God or practicing some discipline to strengthen my spirit in sustained presence. Other times, I would learn about the intricacies of God's heart. In some seasons, I made great strides but found that I could not always maintain the same pace. All of a sudden, the terrain would become steeper and I ended up moving slower.

Then a major change occurred.

I became the land and the treasure transferred into me. Early on He told me what would be a secret to my life, showing me the divine nature of God and my path to ownership in these verses:

> Grace and peace be multiplied to you in the knowledge of God
> and of Jesus our Lord, as His divine power has give to us all things

that pertain to life and godliness, through the knowledge of Him who called us by glory and virtue, by which have been given to us exceedingly great and precious promises, that through these you may be partakers of the divine nature, having escaped the corruption that is in the world through lust. (2 Peter 1:2–4)

The title to the land came with the title to my soul. I could only unlock the land through my believing as well as my dying to self.

I thought knowing God face-to-face on earth would mean encountering miracles and experiencing glowing faces like Moses. Because I had a very specific idea of what a face-to-face relationship with God could look like on earth, this coincided with the expression of my ministry. When my ministry did not go as planned, it challenged my identity. (I didn't know for years that my earthly expression on earth was not necessarily my reception in heaven. I didn't know that access to enjoyment did not mean immediate access to employment.)

Years turned into decades.

I was still in pursuit of the treasure but what was it that I was seeking? Marriage and children had impacted my search. My dreams for the children, our ministry and home became mixed up in my search for intimacy with God. Why did I start this journey? What was I thinking? (I have joked many times that the kingdom of heaven is like a man who finds a treasure in a field, hides it and goes to buy the field. However, when he comes back, he can't find where he buried the treasure.)

Renewal is the essence of rediscovery through the Holy Spirit and His goodness of what has been lost. His goodness revealed, inside or out, opens our minds to repentance and fresh perspective. All of a sudden we remember what the Lord has spoken and where we hid the treasure.

When I discovered intimacy in prayer, I perceived its value and made choices to purchase this field of fellowship with God in the Spirit. I hid it there and went to purchase the land but, with the demands of the immediate and the tyranny of the urgent, time wore thin the decision made in glory. Soon, prayer was only a practice of something that had once opened me to the discovery of face-to-face living. I had lost the map to the treasure.

Yet, the Lord does not leave us in that place. Renewal is Him coming alongside us, listening to our confusion. When that happens, He reinterprets for us the journey we have been on in the light of His word and Holy Spirit. And what happens? We sell the farm again.

Core Scriptures:
2 Peter 1:2–4; Romans 2:4–5; Matthew 6:5–8; Luke 24:13–35

10

FINDING LOST TREASURE

We are God's field. We are His buildings. We become what we have sold everything to gain.

The treasure I saw in the field was a face-to-face relationship with God. I found it in the context of experiences, books, testimonies and many other places. I hid the treasure and went to buy the field in which I had found the treasure.

I prayed and practiced, following the instructions of others with the Holy Spirit as I read His word. He would communicate promises to me (those nods of God) and my heart would respond, "I would give anything to know this..." or "I hope one day to walk in this." These were moments of exchange where I would find treasure in God's word, in messages heard and in fellowship with the Father, where He would promise me my inheritance.

You begin in the field where you found the promise. Then you become the field as you become the promise. The dwelling of God's word in us makes us become the dwelling place of God in us. His word and Spirit are inseparable. As Jesus is in the Father, so we are in Him and He is in us. We are being made perfect in One. The Spirit of God communicates God to us and we discover Him and His knowledge through promises.

All promises have context (the field where we discovered them). Now, we must buy that field and, in buying it, we become the context for the promise. We become God's field.

Our spirit has been born again and our inner man is the field where the treasure is hidden. Mary, the mother of Jesus, heard all the amazing (and sometimes bewildering) stories about Jesus and hid those words in her heart.

We also hide the word in our heart. We can lose sight of the treasure and be unsure of the reward; time and troubles take their toll upon us. This death looks like our loss (yet it is really our gain). We endure light afflictions (because of the word) as the thief comes to steal the word hidden in our heart and weeds grow up to choke the word from becoming fruitful.

In this death, we enter into renewal of the inner man. This happens as we watch His word, which is invisible:

> Therefore we do not lose heart. Even though our outward man is perishing, yet the inward man in being renewed day by day. For our light affliction, which is but for a moment, is working for us a far more exceeding and eternal weight of glory, while we do not look at the things which are seen, but at the things which are not seen. For the things which are seen are temporary, but the things which are not seen are eternal. (2 Corinthians 4:16–18)

We live in two worlds: the natural and the supernatural, the temporary and the eternal, in this life and in Christ. God's promises to us (and the trials that follow) liberate our lives from this context and place them in the context of God's field.

Again, we are His workmanship. We are His field. We are His building. When I pray, I enter into the presence behind the veil where Christ, our forerunner, has gone. I come into His life (from the dead) and into His truth which exists in eternity.

In eternity, everything is in Christ who has redeemed us out of every tongue, tribe, people and nation, and has made us a kingdom of priests to reign on earth. Heaven is coming to earth through you and me. God dwells in us, renewing us day by day, even though our outward man is perishing.

Take heart. You can't lose the treasure because the treasure is in you and me. We are its earthen vessels.

Core Scriptures:
1 Corinthians 3:9; Ephesians 2:11–22; John 17:21; Luke 2:19, 51;
2 Corinthians 4:16–18

11

RECOVERING LOST TREASURE

When the Lord showed me His divine nature and communicated how I would partake of it through His precious promises, I thought, *Cool.* I didn't really know what that meant. I had much to work out, much loss to consider rubbish and many encounters with God to recalibrate my values and worth.

In short, the impartation of the divine nature of God happens one promise at a time and one rediscovery at a time. Partaking of His divine nature means finding, losing, recovering, renewing and finally becoming the promise. God's nods, His voice and word to us are not accidental or ever forgotten by God. They are sent to be accomplished and will not return to Him void. He may speak into the millennial, but still looks for us to hold fast in faith, and let patience perfect its work in us, making us complete.

The Father will continue to speak, promise and give life in His presence as long as we are willing to come and sit with Him. But the demands of this life may impose false definitions of His faithfulness and truth. We see a life of freedom and do not realize that it will come in Christ through our captivity. We become utterly confused at the disparity between our circumstances and His promises.

Still, the word received is the compass setting when the storms of life blow hard against that given word. We hold fast our compass setting, continuing on course, our faith strong and patience alive. In this, time is God's gift to us because it allows us to discover eternity in the temporal and infinity in the finite, one day at a time.

So, day after day, as we hold fast to our faith, let patience have its perfect work and make payments on our field, we actually exhaust ourselves and lose the treasure—which is part of the plan!

An honest heart never goes unrewarded.

I heard this long ago and have proven it true so many times in my life. The problem is that it takes time for the truth of my heart to be known so that I can be honest about the boulder (my stony heart) or the plank (my wrong vision). "Deep calls to deep at the noise of Your waterfalls; all Your waves and billows have gone over me." (Psalm 42:7)

Renewal is the coming of the Lord in sounds of depth, calling to our depth, when we have been living on the surfaces of life. When He does, it is falling in love again, joy and laughter, tears and weeping. It is a discovery of what has been lost.

Renewal comes in seasons and in movements. It should always be welcomed. I can always tell when I am becoming tight in my spirit because I start living in the flesh. Still, no one can convince me that I am living in the flesh because I get deceived into believing my effort counts toward something great. I become goal-oriented and achievement-driven and, ask Cammy, a pain to live with.

My dryness may drive me back to the living waters or His kindness may break through my closed door. However renewal comes, I must drink freely if I am ever to continue the journey till the end. Renewal is coming back into love with Jesus, experiencing His finished work once more, without needing anything else in place of it. All of a sudden, we are found and can answer, "Here I am."

Who is Jesus to you?

Has He become a means to an end other than Himself? When that happens, whatever we are seeking—whether healing, revival or salvation for nations—we have moved away from Him, falling away from our first love.

It was love that started our journey with Christ and gave us the grace to lose everything without attachment. When that love wanes, the journey becomes confusing, disappointing and sad from all our losses. The beauty of God is that the moment we discover our waning love, we are at the door of recovery.

Core Scriptures:
2 Peter 1:2–4; Philippians 3:7–11; James 1:2–4; 1 Timothy 1:18;
Matthew 7:1–5; Psalm 104:30; 51:10–11

12

ABIDE IN ME

Jesus said, "Abide in Me, and I in you. As the branch cannot bear fruit of itself, unless it abides in the vine, neither can you, unless you abide in Me," (John 15:4)

Thank God for this scripture. It's a silly thought, thanking God for His word. Actually, though, it's not a silly thought at all. Thanking God for His word is faith alive. Gratitude is the fruit of grace and grace is the fruit of faith.

Where are we in our journey?

From conception to birth, from believing to receiving, beginning to ending, so much space can exist. There are many pitfalls along the way: immaturity of the Spirit, earthly longings that lust against the Spirit, and, oh yes, betrayal.

Staring in the face of our human failures and our own personal shortcomings, there is the law ever-present in some form to show us how we *should have* lived. If we could only have lived, done, been, etc., then God would have honored His promises to us.

I cannot tell you how many times I have fallen for this lie because it is tempting to consider yourself smart enough to be part of the equation of salvation. Promises made are inheritances given and are not dependent upon the law.

Long before God reveals any promise to us, He has already determined within Himself His ability to deliver that promise. The promise is not conditional upon our ability but is complete in Christ and brought through us by faith. "For if the inheritance is of the law, it is no longer of promise; but God gave it to Abraham by promise," (Galatians 3:18)

The problem is that promises are contended over. The thief comes to take what has been sown in our hearts. Brothers become jealous of our privileged words. We bumble along, ever confident in our flesh that we know what is next or what we need to do, if only given the chance.

So, a promise given to us from heaven becomes a point of contention, jealousy or work while, at the same time, carrying the nature and eternity of God in itself! We receive His promise and His nature takes hold but we are still living in our old nature—striving, fearing and reacting.

Now we are in the God drama. The harder we work, the harder we fall. The more we run, the faster we are pursued. The longer we refuse, the more we are out-waited by God. It is really impossible to be separated from His love. Eventually, we come to see that our perceptions, fears, and old nature must die.

I'm describing my own struggles here. I have yet to learn that it has all been given to me, that my sonship is assured and that I am fully accepted in the Beloved. Well yes, I know this but I don't *know* it—because I must gain this knowledge experientially after I fail at my own attempts at ownership and achievement.

The fact is that I must try to do the word for the word to come alive. I must try to keep the word for the word to keep me because it is only when I give myself to become what I have been promised that the promise takes deep root into my spirit and resurrection is assured.

You see the promises that you have heard (and yes, you have heard the Lord speak to you). You may be in a dark valley with so little light that it has crowded out the euphoria you had when you first heard the promise or the simple peace and joy resulting from the thought of His love for you (which is promise in itself). Anytime the revelation of God (the seeing) comes, promise of its continuance and future maturity accompanies it.

God doesn't just happen by, spill some love, light or life on you and then say, "Whoops, I didn't really mean anything by that. That was for the other guy." No. God is intentional. He touches us, drawing us with desire. The smallest thought towards God is a promise of life with Him. A whisper of His presence is a river of eternity in His love. Yes. You have been given promises!

Core Scriptures:
2 Peter 1:2–4; Romans 8:31–39; Mathew 16:13–20; Philippians 1:6;
Ephesians 1:4-6

13

THE DIVINE NATURE OF GOD

Promises are seeds. Once sown, they begin to take over everything. Like yeast in bread dough, they grow until the whole loaf rises. Promises, whispers of God's love and desires for His attention initiate a transfer of ownership of ourselves from self to God. Our domain name changes from earth to heaven. Our destiny changes from wandering to a life that is promise-fulfilled.

It is just going to take some time.

Promises carry our destinies but they carry much more than that—they carry the divine nature of God. They are *His* seed sown into our hearts and they begin our journey of separation from this world to the adherence to the image and likeness of His Son.

This does not happen at first. Initially, we pretty much hear just the promise and move towards it within our current understanding and values. That's why the process of the promises of God is a cleansing process, one which recalibrates and brings about the renewal of our minds.

Peace and joy accompany His voice when you hear the whisper of His goodness toward you or the sense of His encouragement to believe this about that. He speaks and we sense His kingdom, righteousness, peace, and joy. We receive and conceive His kingdom within our spirits.

In this, we are the dwelling place of God in the Spirit through our hearing and keeping His word. Yet, "keeping" is not the outward observance of His word. It is the watching of His word. The promise itself is the answer, not the completion of it.

In His presence, He calls things that do not exist as though they do—because, in the unseen realm where God dwells, they do exist. You may not know you're pregnant with His word, just like a young mother may not yet know she is pregnant, but she will know. You will know too.

The promise constrains us, invisibly at first, changing priorities, even habits, but later it takes over our very future. Because it is the process of the unseen overtaking the seen, it may not appear at all like the promise is coming to pass. In fact, many times it will look like the opposite of that promise.

Peter saw that Jesus was the Christ. Upon this revelation Jesus changed his name from Simon to Peter (a reed to a rock). Jesus promised that He would build His church and gave Peter the keys to the kingdom. After Jesus commended Peter for receiving this revelation from the Father, He began to reveal to his disciples His coming sufferings, death and resurrection. Peter, taking the Lord aside, rebuked Him, saying it would never come to pass. Jesus turned and said to Peter,

> Get behind me, Satan, you are an offense to Me, for you are not mindful of the things of God, but the things of men. (Matthew 16:23b)

What happened here? Peter received revelation but interpreted it in a human context, instead of a godly one. Said another way, the promise was there but the divine nature had not yet developed within him.

Jesus used this moment to share that God's promises require self-denial. His followers must take up their cross and follow Him. He was revealing that promise would create conflict and circumstances that would lead to the death of the soul life before resurrection.

At His return in the glory of His Father with His angels, there would be incredible rewards for such a pilgrimage. Jesus went on, saying that some of His disciples would not taste death till they saw Jesus coming in His kingdom.

Well, six days later, Peter, James and John experienced just that when Jesus took them up on a high mountain, and there, transfigured before them, with Moses and Elijah appearing and speaking together with Christ regarding His departure.

This is what the fulfilled promise will do. It will transfigure you.

Core Scriptures:
Hebrews 11:16; Romans 12:1–2; Romans 14:17; Romans 4:17;
Luke 1:34–38, 45; Mathew 16:13–28; 17:1–13

14

THE CONSTRAINING POWER OF GOD

You are so loved. You don't know it. I barely know it, even after so much death to my soul life, but we are so loved. In His presence, there is a glory realm where His promises and our tears are kept together—because they represent the word of God unchangeable and the pain of the death of our soul life.

I say "soul life" because that is what it is. It is the life we live within our soul that derives its identity and value from the so-called "things of man." Joseph was greatly loved by his father, Jacob. He was highly favored, you might say. Joseph had a coat of many colors (which set him apart from his eleven brothers) and the special treatment that went along with it.

His brothers were jealous of him and, when he began sharing his promises (the dreams he had of them bowing down to him), they could no longer tolerate him. Fortunately, they were out feeding the flocks while Joseph was at home.

Still the time came when, his brothers, provoked by Joseph's favored status and dreams of greatness, sent Joseph to Egypt. Although it was ultimately God's intentionality to save nations that sent Joseph to Egypt, from Joseph's perspective, he found himself looking up into the faces of his brothers from a pit that they had thrown him in.

He pleaded with them to get him out but to no avail. Rather, they sat down to eat. When they saw a caravan of Ishmaelites headed to Egypt, the brothers decided not to murder Joseph but to sell him as a slave. So Joseph, crying, begging and pleading with his brothers, was shipped off as a slave of the Ishmaelites. Off to Egypt he went.

Potiphar, the captain of the guard and an officer of Pharaoh, bought Joseph. Frightened, Joseph did what he was told. It was not long before Potiphar saw that the Lord was with Joseph and prospering everything he put in his hand. (God's word is eternal, as are His promises to us. Once spoken, God jealously watches over them.)

Joseph was grateful to the Lord for His being there with him, blessing his work and giving him favor in the sight of Potiphar. He was retaining the promise in a situation of great adversity. Hope lived in Joseph and he knew there would be change and deliverance.

After some time, Potiphar's wife "cast longing eyes upon Joseph and said 'lie with me.'" (Genesis 39:7b) Joseph refused, saying it would be a great sin against his master (her husband) and against God. But that didn't stop her. Day after day, she pursued him. Day after day, Joseph held his integrity. (Promises bring out the best in us—because they are hope and they purify us. Promises make us better people. We choose good and do well. We refuse evil but, as we are about to see with Joseph, we do not always receive the same treatment.)

Potiphar's wife finally caught Joseph alone in her house. She demanded, "Lie with me," while grasping his garment in her hand.

"No," Joseph said. He fled, leaving his garment in her hand. She had once again been refused. Her passion turning to anger, she decided to do away with him. Joseph was panic-stricken. What would happen? How could this be happening to him?

Little did he know things were about to get a lot worse.

How would you train a man to become a prime minister of a nation, destined to save nations and fulfill promises you had made four generations before?

I wouldn't think that you would sow that man, that seed of promise, deep into the dungeons of Egypt to be abused, accused, imprisoned and forgotten. But that is exactly what God did with Joseph. We wonder. What about the person carrying the promise? What would that do to him? Could he endure such an ordeal?"

God knows all things. He utters His word, confident that He is able to bring it to pass without our ability. He is a God that doesn't make promises that He is not willing or unable to fulfill.

Core Scriptures:
Genesis 37; 39; 15:13–16; Acts 7:6–10; Romans 4:21

15

FURTHER IN AND FURTHER UP

Further in and further up in the kingdom is usually deeper in and deeper down in the earthly realm. Joseph sure found that out. When Potiphar came home, his wife accused Joseph of trying to rape her. Enraged, Potiphar sent Joseph into the dungeons of Pharaoh—as a prisoner with no recourse or hope of escape.

Still, as Joseph stared into the darkness of his prison cell, the Lord was with him. Every tumble down is a step up in the kingdom, even when we cannot see it. Joseph wasn't seeing it and he sure wasn't feeling it.

But Joseph maintained his integrity. Like Job, he held his innocence and waited for God to deliver him. Until then, he continued to serve. Joseph had the first prison ministry in the Bible and soon he was in charge of the entire prison. Everything that was done in the prison was his doing:

> The keeper of the prison did not look into anything that was under Joseph's authority, because the Lord was with him; and whatever he did, the Lord made it prosper. (Genesis 39:23)

This was so important and took a lot of time. Why? God placed Joseph deep into the darkest recesses of Egypt to embed the seed of

His promise deeply into this man. God's promise went past the feeling of, "Wow, God is going to use me," and "I will hold my integrity even in this injustice," and even past the feeling, "I will walk with God here in the darkest of situations, for He will deliver me."

Rather, setback after setback, disappointment after disappointment drove the promise deeper into Joseph's spirit. His soul soon lost hope and became fixated upon injustice. His efforts were winding down. If only he could just get out of this prison. What had he done to deserve such treatment?

God never leaves us alone. While Joseph's soul was dying amid all those dying promises, the Lord would bring hints of hope, just enough awakening that Joseph would come alive again. That is what the butler brought—a hope of deliverance.

By that time, Joseph couldn't hide his own pain and death. He told on himself, his moment of hope crystallized his soul's anguish, and injustice turned to bitterness. He had finally come to the end of his efforts to keep the promise alive. "I just want to get out of here. I just want to go home," were his innermost cries.

The butler's dream, rightly interpreted by Joseph, led to a glimmer of hope: *If this butler will show me kindness when he is restored in three days to his chief of staff position to Pharaoh, then maybe I can get home again*, Joseph thought. So he blurted out his prayer to the Pharaoh's butler, "But remember me when it is well with you, and please show kindness to me; make mention of me to Pharaoh, and get me out of this house. For indeed I was stolen away from the land of the Hebrews; and also I have done nothing here that they should put me into the dungeon." (Genesis 40:14–15)

But of course, that was not God's plan of deliverance. God would not let a man open a door He had so purposefully shut. It would not be as Joseph had hoped. He would not be released. Joseph would not return home to disintegrate the family and make God's promises to Abraham and Isaac untrue. No. Joseph must stay where he was; the promise was not going to abide alone—it had to die. Being set free was not God's plan for Joseph, even if it was Joseph's plan for himself.

Joseph, no longer able to keep the word, his life ebbing away, could only see relief as the answer. The butler was released and rose back to his position. But Joseph stayed where he was, in prison, left and forgotten.

Core Scriptures:
Job 4:6; Genesis 40; John 12:24; Psalm 94

16

DEATH OF A VISION

The death of a vision is not the death of the eternal word but the death of our soul life. It is the part of us that first cultivated the vision, entertained, felt and lived it in our imagination. Now with the death of our soul life, we can see only darkness. All we feel is pain. We resign ourselves to believing that things will never change.

Why would God do this? What purpose could be gained for His kingdom by allowing us to die? It is not unto death but for the glory of God! Yes, we die but not forever. Truly, like Lazarus, we are dead in the grave and without hope but God isn't. With His voice, the resurrection and the life of Jesus Christ will awaken the dead.

In those moments, the promise that initiated our abandonment to the Lord and the subsequent journey is no longer in the picture. We find ourselves alone with God saying, "I can't trust you."

I remember feeling at one point that I had heard so much from the Spirit of the Lord in promises, words, prophecies, visions and dreams that I felt I couldn't go on. What was it about the Lord that I had misunderstood? Did I misinterpret what He said? Did I fail to obey Him or fail to do my part to fulfill His promise?

Questions, doubts, and more doubts fill our minds. Our soul, now left alone, no longer alive with the word's hope, must face its death. Our soul has not and is not able to bring the word to pass. It is not noble, smart or strong enough. Relief is all that we want.

How long we are here probably has as much to do with how hard we tried or how great we were in our own minds. But who knows? It just seems like forever as, little by little, hope of salvation is given up and resignation to the situation takes hold. Then we wonder, *What now? What if I never get out? What if the promise is never fulfilled? Does this make God a liar; can I force Him to do His word?* Little by little, our ownership is transferred. The word of promise is His and the outcome, too.

Freedom comes when you no longer need the promise to be fulfilled in order to believe God—when you no longer need the circumstances to change in order to enjoy God. Instead, a new place has been found—contentment. It is not resignation (because resignation still carries bitterness). It is enjoyment in God in the place you find yourself. Unable to deliver yourself, you find enjoyment in God apart from your circumstances.

It is the journey of promise. We waited patiently when we saw fulfillment of the promise coming. We continued waiting when we saw its fulfillment delayed. We may have even continued when we saw fulfillment denied, thinking it would eventually turn around.

Then it dawns on us that it may never turn around and that we may always be in this same difficult situation. Now what? Do I live in prison to my denied promise, unable to trust and enjoy God, or do I reconcile this enigma back to God and live again?

At some point, the prospect of freedom from the internal prison becomes more enticing than the thought of recovery or rescue from the external prison. So we begin looking for internal freedom and, as the Lord takes full control, we are at peace and at rest. What we do not know, however, is that we are about to enter into the most fulfilling point of the pilgrimage of our faith.

You are going to enter into the presence behind the veil to live, move and exist there—to enjoy and receive what you do not have (because now you do not need to receive to believe), you simply believe you have received.

It's not a play on words—it's a translation of citizenship from earth to heaven. You no longer belong here. Your home is the city that has foundations whose Builder and Maker is God. You are in the New Jerusalem before its earthly landing; you have become a dwelling place for God in the Spirit.

Core Scriptures:
Luke 2:34–35; John 11:1–14; Psalms 42; 73; Hebrews 11:13–16

17

A PILGRIM IN THE LAND OF PROMISE

Abraham obeyed God by faith. He left the land of his ancestors and went out without knowing where he was going. He dwelt in tents in the land of promise with Isaac and Jacob, heirs of the same promise, because he was looking for a city whose builder and maker was God.

God is always looking for men and women with whom He can share what He is doing before He does it. God is pleased when He finds someone who is willing to hear His voice, workings and movements. Someone who is able to maintain faith throughout God's endeavors. The Lord has no problem with what He has said, what has happened or what has failed to happen. His word is truth. He is fully able to execute His promises and complete His word, long after we have heard, tried, failed and moved on.

While coming into this acceptance and understanding, I asked the Father about Abraham: "Why did Abraham please you so much? What made Abraham your friend?" The reply I got shocked but also greatly helped me. I heard the Father say, "I found in Abraham a man who would listen to Me and believe Me without requiring fulfillment as a condition of trust. Abraham did not stop listening and I did not stop talking."

The Father went on to say with enthusiasm in His voice, "Most men demand sight at some point in their journey with Me. When that is not possible, they stop listening, struggle with My existence, intentions or goodness. Drawing back, they cease to want to hear." *Wow,* I thought. Imagine God having a hard time being able to talk with anyone His heart desires because of our own disappointments and need for completion.

I hit a vein of communication that day, because the Father wanted to talk more with me about this. "Imagine Abraham, the father of faith, to whom three quarters of the world's religions adhere to as father of their faith. He never owned for himself a piece of the promise, only his grave site," the Father said to me. He continued, "Consider how that would look today." Abraham died without possessing the Promised Land.

Yet, he saw it far off and had embraced it. In so doing, he said he was a stranger and pilgrim on the earth. I looked at Hebrews 11:14–16: "for those who say such things declare plainly that they seek a homeland. And truly if they had called to mind that country from which they had come out, they would have had opportunity to return. But now they desire a better, that is, a heavenly country. Therefore God is not ashamed to be called their God, for He has prepared a city for them."

Abraham was God's friend, because Abraham allowed God to call things that did not exist as though they did. He never made God prove anything. Abraham made his one attempt to fulfill God's promise and had a child through Hagar, since all rational thought said that Sarai (Sarah before her name was changed) could never have a child because she was barren. After that he didn't try again.

Abraham lived in the Promised Land in the midst of incomplete circumstances.

The Father concluded that day's talk to me with this promise: "I will speak to a man as far and wide as he is able to listen and believe. When he is freed from his need to see and have, he enters into another realm—into mine. Unlimited by his life's ability, unhindered by his failures, he listens and he believes and I can speak freely. I have very few men or women who will let Me speak to them beyond their ability to obtain. But when I find one...I talk a lot."

Core Scriptures:
Hebrews 11:8–12; Romans 4:17; Hebrews 6:13–20; Acts 7:5; Genesis 15

18

IN THE PRESENCE

Imagine how many of God's promises are meant to be enjoyed in His presence long before they are ever seen on earth. In the presence of Him who calls things into existence, the Lord invites us to enjoy Him in His promises. It is here that we hold fast to our confession of hope, without wavering, for He is faithful who has promised.

David said in Psalm 16:11: "In Your presence is fullness of joy; at Your right hand are pleasures forevermore." David discovered that the Lord is alive and vibrant, that He is the one who we are to fellowship with inside of promise, allowing God to speak outside of our life's circumstances.

God places us inside of Himself. He speaks to us in Christ, beyond our immediate experience or pay grade. We are included into the very workings of God. Some will manifest in our lifetime while others will not. Even others may be prophetic declarations of Christ in His coming.

Let's consider what came of David's encounter with God. In the second chapter of Acts, Peter stood up on the day of Pentecost and explained the process of baptism in the Holy Spirit with writings from the prophet Joel. Then he went on to explain the resurrection using David's Psalm 16.

Let's listen in on Peter as he gave the message that morning:

> For David says concerning Him: "I foresaw the Lord always before my face, for He is at my right hand, that I may not be shaken.
>
> Therefore my heart rejoiced, and my tongue was glad; moreover my flesh also will rest in hope. For You will not leave my soul in Hades, nor will you allow Your Holy One to see corruption. You have made known to me the ways of life; You will make me full of joy in Your presence."
>
> Men and brethren let me speak freely to you of the patriarch David that he is both dead and buried and his tomb is with us to this day. Therefore, being a prophet and knowing that God had sworn an oath to him that of the fruit, of his body according to the flesh, He would raise up the Christ to sit on his throne, he, foreseeing this, spoke concerning the resurrection of the Christ, that His soul was not left in Hades nor did His flesh see corruption. (Acts 2:25–31)

What was happening here? David saw the promise in the first person: "You will not leave my soul in Hades nor will you allow Your Holy One to see corruption." David was living in the presence of the Lord, moving in between promises of God for Him and for Christ, stepping in and out of the temporal and eternal.

This happens all the time in the Spirit but we get all messed up when we try to bring all that we have heard back into our temporal world.

What if David had insisted he was not going to die or that he would be raised from the dead? David would have been right in Christ but wrong in his lifetime.

David just enjoyed the moment, wrote down the promise, and closed with, "You will show me the path of life; in Your presence is fullness of joy; at Your right hand are pleasures forevermore." (Psalm 16:11)

You see, God is always speaking, declaring His comings and goings. Can we be His receiver on this earth, recording His word to us, allowing it to flow out of us, without making it about ourselves? Can we sing beyond our present victory and sing into the future victories experiencing the joy set before us? Can we carry promises that are beyond our understanding or fulfillment?

We can, when we are dead to our sense of self life, overcome in His joy. In both places, there is an elevation above this life into the very workings of God. There, like the words of the Song of Moses, we can sing of victories beyond our lifetime. Like David with the song of his deliverance (Psalm 18), we can sing about dimensions of victories no mortal can see.

Core Scriptures:
Romans 4:17; Hebrews 6:18–20; 2 Peter 1:19–21;
Exodus 15:1–21; Psalm 18

19

GOD'S GOAL IS US

We are the Lord's inheritance. He has a calling in us and He will employ all means at His disposal to possess us. He will awaken us to His presence, intoxicating us in His love, speaking words of comfort and greatness, beckoning us to run.

And run we do. One encounter with God can ruin you for a lifetime. It will shift your desire, choices and vision. He is after you with His words, presence, power and promises. He is your destiny and you are His. It is an honor to be called by the Lord. Every word, promise and encounter is an example of His calling us to Himself.

But flesh and blood cannot inherit the kingdom.

In fact, no flesh will glory in His presence, but we have a problem because we are flesh and blood. The very presence and promise that touched us touched all of us (flesh included), moving us with a sense of power and might. We think that the promises we have heard and experienced are ours now or just around the corner!

Still, in many cases, we experience the exact opposite of what we expect. We may boast of our good fortune or tell others of what the Lord said, invoking jealousy or unbelief. And we will use our strength, our resources, our gifts and our abilities; they may have all been given to us by God but they are not God. They must yield to Him.

I remember the day the Lord said to me, "We can't both be strong." Either I would be weak and He would be strong or I would be strong and He would be weak in my life. God dwells in eternity as the high and lofty One but He also dwells with the "contrite and humble spirit" (which literally means "crushed and depressed spirit"). The outward man will not succeed to impress God or find a place before God. It will die.

What is this outward man? It is the image of the first Adam, our "soul life," meaning: our abilities, gifts, talents, personality and will. That's why the cross is so difficult to bear. It crosses our will, ideals or ways. Our soul life will be redeemed but Jesus said, "If you seek to save your soul life you will lose it, but if you lose your soul life for My sake you will find it."

That's right. You will find your life again and it will no longer be merely a living soul but a life-giving spirit.

Jesus Himself said no one could take His life but that He would lay it down and take it again. This is our journey, too. In following Christ, we are required to lay down our natural soul life because it will not be forced from us. Although we may endure many trials and disappointments and, with resolve and willful strength, continue to move forward, eventually we will all die, giving up ever trying to perform the promise or complete the work.

Feeling like failures, we may shrink back from following the Lord or become angry at the sacrifices that we have made for nothing. We might regret our choices, resent those who encouraged us to follow them and even get into a real funk; refusing to be comforted as we pine away in our sorrows.

Believe me. I know.

Core Scriptures:
Ephesians 1:17–18; 1 Corinthians 15:50; Isaiah 57:15;
1 Corinthians 15:45–49; John 10:17–18

20

THE SEED MUST FALL INTO
THE GROUND AND DIE

In 1998, the Lord promised that, within a year's time, Jubilee Church would be in revival. It was an unsolicited word given to me when I asked, "Where will we be this time next year?" I had asked the question of the Lord out of wonderment because of the difficulties of the day (rather than out of faith and expectation). So it really surprised me when the Father said, "This time next year you will be in revival."

Fresh with this promise and the accompanying Holy Spirit, I set out to be where the Lord said we would be in a year's time. Faith began to take hold of everyone as the Spirit of the Lord continued to increase. The water level was rising.

As promised, we entered into revival, but one that could not be sustained—jealousy, legalism, sin, warfare and human frailty had been revived too. By 2000 (only two years after the promise), the church split, leaving people confused and dismayed.

So what happened? Did the Father not tell the whole truth? Did He set me up? Did I sin and miss it or did someone else sin?

The promises simply had to pass through the cross. My efforts, noble as they may have been, would need to be sifted by the devil and tested by God because there is nothing like hope to awaken our selfish ambitions, rights and privileges that lie dormant during periods of drought or famine. It was a divine setup and, yet, it was all true. God was using everything and everyone to conform us to His death so that we might attain to His resurrection.

The promises of God must be believed, received, tried and failed in order to fall into the ground and die – or, more accurately, for us to fall into the ground and die. In this case, we are the seed, our soul life dying to the promise and our imagination of its fulfillment.

This death was awful, painful and slow. It affected so many more people than just me. It affected my children, marriage, church and my ministry as demonic hordes surrounded me and flung their accusations.

The cross is not a place where we die alone but a place of public ridicule, perceived or real. "He trusted God...let Him save Him," and "Come down from there [the cross] and we will believe you," and even "He saved others; let Him save Himself." Jesus heard these accusations as He hung upon the cross. Our soul wants to be right and so we may ask, "Whatever did I do to deserve this? Where is God now...My God, my God; why have You forsaken me?"

Not everyone processes crises in the same way. Some run, while others join the accusations. Even others crumble under the weight and shame. Rebellion, fear, shame and reproach can cloak the cross's heavenly intention of resurrection. Yes, we die but not alone, or easily for that matter, because the natural life has great resilience and resolve.

When our hope in God is crushed, death follows. Yet, to do well and suffer seems so unnecessary to the soul.

This is where disillusionment, distrust, casting blame and everything else can come in. Questions, efforts, and refusals all come but it doesn't matter. Eventually we die to the dream we held and give up hope of the promise. Feeling forsaken, we settle into the conformity to His death.

For me, this took four years, until January 2004, of resisting and denying this death in my soul. I even faked my own death many times. I knew the scriptures, the ways of God and His workings. I would die, but I would hope and keep coming back. I would memorize more scriptures to keep the promises alive. I would pray (Oh, how I prayed) for hours, days, weeks and years, continually coming to the Lord with my life and His promises.

It wasn't as bad as continually saying, "You said," like an impatient child. Rather, my behavior was still an example of religion trying to solve the riddle of what the Lord was doing. Truth was that I was dying. It should have been easy to see but it wasn't. Not to me.

Core Scriptures:
Luke 22:31–34; Matthew 26:31–35; 16:21–27; 27:39–46

21

I LOST MY MARBLES

In the movie *Hook*, Robin Williams plays a grown-up Peter Pan. There is also an elderly gentleman (one of the lost boys) who continually goes around asking everyone, "Have you seen my marbles? I lost my marbles." At the end of the movie when Peter returns to London, he gives the man his marbles, which Peter had recovered in Never-Never Land. With the marbles in hand, the elderly gentleman immediately begins to fly. The marbles were his "happy thought."

In many ways, God's promises allow us to step into His divine nature and escape the corruption that is in this world through lust. Moving from fear to love, in faith, we rise into new places where we can fly in His Spirit. When these promises are taken from us, we are grounded, having lost our "happy thought."

Recovering His promises, when circumstances have gone wrong, is not an easy task. In a sense, we have rejected His word because it made no sense to us. The word of God is not natural or of this world; it is not limited to our understanding or our experience. God's word answers to no man. It explains itself at the revelation of the Father's heart, not our demanding minds.

The word is mixed with faith in the hearer or, otherwise, carries no strength to face giants, or to enter into rest. The word of God is living and alive, discerning the thoughts and intentions of the heart, making all things naked before the Lord. It is glorious and can wash the bride into glorious beauty. It is our salvation by faith and will lift us up above the beggarly elements of this world. Through the word of Jesus, we can walk on water, raise the dead and do anything required of us by God.

During his two years in prison, Joseph had to find his marbles again. Similarly, that was what I had to do also. Because the promises made to Joseph and the experiences that followed were the opposite of what he had expected, Joseph needed to be reconciled back to God. He needed to come out of his funk: "I am a Hebrew who was enslaved. I have done nothing deserving of this prison."

To receive the promises of God again without the baggage of life, Joseph had to let go of a lot of experiences. When Joseph did, he was ready to fly up out of Pharaoh's dungeons into Pharaoh's presence, up into the very heights of power, which far exceeded his expectations. Joseph found his marbles and the Promise Maker – which allowed him to step back into eternity.

I am not sure what happened to him during those last two years in prison but I have an idea because something happened to me during 2010 and 2011. I think, though, it started in earnest on a Wednesday night service somewhere in the early 2000s.

I was teaching the story of Joseph. When I got to the part of his being forgotten and left in prison for two full years, I paused and said out loud, "Wouldn't you give anything to find out what happened to Joseph in his last two years of prison?"

From the front row, Cammy yelled, "No!" She was right.

In order to understand what happened to Joseph, you would have to have had a similar experience. You would have to be familiar with promises gone awry, impossible circumstances and a fierce longing for relief. Well, I don't know if the Lord didn't listen to Cammy's protest that night, or if I was too stubborn to hear, but I began the descent into hopelessness.

I lost my marbles.

Core Scriptures:
2 Peter 1:2–4; Job 38:1–7; Hebrews 4:2; Ephesians 5:26-27;
Genesis 41:14–16

22

FIGHTING BACK

Death is an enemy—the last one that will be put under our feet—and comes in all forms and sizes. Jesus destroyed the Devil, who had the power of death in order to free us who were enslaved to the fear of death. In other words, the fear of death is as great as death or, even worse, because it carries bondage within it.

My first inclination toward death came in the early 2000s as our church's revival (and the promises yet to be fulfilled) began to move farther and farther away from my grasp. I went to prayer, pressing the Lord on His promises and demanding that He keep His word.

For three days, I did not stop reminding the Lord of His covenant— that He could not lie, nor would I relent. I took the posture of the widow and He was the unjust judge. Every day, I came and demanded that He bring fulfillment, restoration and redemption.

Finally, He spoke to me, "If you keep pressing Me to fulfill My promises to you, I will, but many will be lost. If you will be patient and wait, many more will be saved."

The Lord had my attention. Truth was, it was a part of Him catching me in my own craftiness and integrity. Of course I would wait but to wait was frustrating. Still, what was I supposed to do—behave self-ishly and demand that God fulfill His word, without caring that doing so would result in something that wasn't His best effort? No. I would be a good boy, maybe a little like Joseph—unwilling to com-promise his character and sin against God. I said "No" to the "mis-tress of lust."

The Lord said, "No." I said, "No." And all hell broke loose.

I don't know how things are worked out in the kingdom of God. Each of us has our own story, but we can hear mistakes or errors of judgment made by others and smugly say, "That's stupid." It may be but, "Stupid is as stupid does," Forrest Gump's mom would always say to him. So when you do something stupid, it is the choice of the moment, not necessarily the lifetime.

In my mind, I wasn't doing anything stupid but, in a way, I was behaving ridiculously. I answered God's request to be patient with, "If I cannot force this into being now, then I am going to fill the atmosphere with the word of God, the promises He has made that are yet to be fulfilled." In hindsight, it seemed noble but I was only behaving more willfully, just like Joseph in his prison.

Pressing God's promises into the atmosphere had an enlivening effect. I memorized whole chapters of the Bible. All His promises were "yes and amen" in Christ, and they had been whispered into my heart, spoken into my spirit and given to me by God. There was no mistaking that I had heard God. His voice was a whisper, nod or go-ahead. The Holy Spirit's encouragement was awesomely effective.

As Moses found out, once you turn to see the bush burning, God has got you. He begins to speak, you begin to believe and eternity is sown into your heart. So, every morning, I would go down to the church for prayer, filling the sanctuary with chapters and verses, images of faith and declarations of His word.

I began going through my journals, looking back over years, highlighting promises, extrapolating words and putting them all into a new book called *Divine Promises*. I was implanting the word of God deep in my soul.

I was still in control. Or, so I thought.

Core Scriptures:
Hebrews 2:14–15; Luke 18:1–8; 2 Corinthians 1:20; Exodus 3:1–4

23

LOSING MY PLACE

For two to three years, I held these words alive in my soul. By the end of 2003, I had memorized many chapters and encounters in the Bible. I was much like the father in the movie, *Holes*.

In *Holes*, Henry Winkler plays a father who is obsessed with discovering a formula that will prevent shoes from stinking. Throughout the film, you see him feverishly working in the kitchen over the stove, adding ingredients, and thinking that *this* time he had the right formula. All the while, his wife, son and father sat at the kitchen table, unimpressed and tired of the never-ending process.

When we saw this movie, Cammy said, "That's you. You're always seeking to obtain from God something He has promised. You go back each time, trying a new formula in prayer, declaration and faith—adding a little of this and a little more of that." She was right. My efforts, to honor God and keep His word, had grown into an obsession—one without trust.

Then, one morning in January 2004, I was kneeling down next to my chair and I heard the Lord pronounce the scripture, "Most assuredly, I say to you, unless a grain of wheat falls into the ground and dies, it remains alone; but if it dies, it produces much grain." (John 12:24) The phrase, "but if it dies," resounded in me. God will often quote His word; it is the sword of the Spirit, and when He does, it comes alive with faith and authority.

That's why I often remember exactly where I am, the time of day, even the look and feel of the room or place that I am in when God speaks to me. It is like a picture is taken. The moment is frozen and marked in eternity.

The phrase, "but if it dies," came alive and, with it, came understanding. I heard the Father say, "You haven't allowed the seed to die. It has fallen into the ground, but you must let it die if it is to bear much fruit."

In that moment, I said, "The revival is dead." This was the summation of all the promises as I understood them. I gave away all the scriptures that I had memorized to finally let the word fall into the ground and die. It was an amazing release because I no longer held the responsibility to bring the promises to pass by my faith and confession. My efforts to hold the word had broken down my soul. But now, I was free!

I went home and told Cammy, "The revival is dead." She said, "I know that. It has been dead for four years." OK. So I am a slow learner. That is the problem with promise, faith, prayer and effort—they become convoluted. It is so much easier to focus on performing good works instead of staying in faith and rest.

The rest of that year became an amazing time of reconciling myself to all that had happened, and with the specific promise of "bearing much fruit." I was alive again—watching, waiting and looking for the fulfillment of promise with "much fruit."

Like Joseph, I had more sideways hits, more setbacks and doors closing rather than opening. It is funny because, in life, we do the same thing over and over again until something sets us into a new course. It is not so much that we are unwilling to change, but rather we just lack the opportunity.

During the next few years, I would think of Joseph often, sitting in that dungeon and losing hope as the years went by. Maybe he happened to get a copy of the Hebrew prophetic journal. Reading the journal, he saw that there was a great move coming—a move of God on earth. Nations would change and merge.

There were words about the promises given to Abraham regarding Egypt and exhortations to get ready, be prepared and move forward together into the destiny that was unfolding. However, there Joseph sat in a dungeon without the freedom to move. He was unable to get ready or participate. What could he do?

Often, when God's promises are dying (or we are dying), the voices around us say, "You need to do something." But you already tried doing so much that you are finally settling down and letting go of making the effort. This doesn't mean that you feel free—rather, you feel defeated.

You are giving up, something you told yourself you would never do.

Core Scriptures:
John 12:24–26; Ezekiel 1:1–3; Daniel 10:4–9; Acts 27:21

24

BESIDES, YOU'RE THE PASTOR

What's the purpose in keeping faith in the word and holding out for its fulfillment if we have to die first anyway? Why not die immediately and be done with it—just quit trying now and shorten the process?

The time we spend holding His word, contending for it, does so many things for us. For one, the promise goes deeper and deeper into our being as we hold the words of eternal life. You can't throw away eternal life, so you keep it, trying to make it come forth. In 2005, I began making plans to write this book. I planned to call it *The Place between Two Worlds*. It was a picture of living in promise without fulfillment, kind of a limbo place. It was not a passive existence because I was continually trying to "be a part of the fulfillment."

God's promises need time to take root. When disappointment comes, it is easy to let go of the word. During this time, I was thankful I had to continue to minister His word and pastor His church because it forced me to get into the Spirit every week. I had to separate my soul and minister His word apart from my circumstances. Finding God while serving, ministering and standing, was a training exercise. I didn't know what I was training for but I kept on.

I was like the man waking up on Sunday morning to his wife encouraging him to get ready for church. "I'm not going to church this Sunday," he said. "Why dear?" was his wife's kind and nudging reply. "I don't know. I don't get anything out of it," he replied gruffly. "Give me four reasons I should get up and go to church today." His wife answered, "Well, that's not true, you do hear from God when you go, and you're always glad you went when we get home." He answered, "Yeah, but that's only two reasons. Give me two more." "OK," she said, a bit tired of this game, "You enjoy worshipping God; it brings you into His presence. And besides, you're the pastor."

Well, that was me. Cammy never had to resort to actually convincing me to go but, since I was the pastor, I went and would encounter God. I would hear His voice and feel better.

Continuing in the work is a crucial part of transformation. You can't just believe, die to self-effort and resurrect in one service or one year for that matter. No. You will walk through a pilgrimage like Abraham, Isaac, Jacob, David and all the patriarchs. Staying in the work ensures you don't separate yourself from God by casting away your faith. Faith works. It serves, gives, believes and continues in patience.

After all, you never know when God's promise will be fulfilled. If I knew back then what I know now, I would have been much more patient but worked just as hard. I was building in the Spirit or, more correctly, I was being built in the Spirit to be a habitation of God. Through His promises, God was imparting His very nature into me, building within me a place of dwelling for the Father and the Son by the Holy Spirit, a house upon the Rock.

My soul had its interpretation of the promises and purposes for such wonderful visions. In such difficult experiences, I would hold my place even as I was losing my place. I learned to live in the Spirit, not in my soul. More and more, I would find God apart from my circumstances. I would live in the place between two worlds, not in limbo, but in the Holy Spirit.

Deep cried out to deep at the sound of His waters. I stopped my secret formulas. I was living in a place of grace, content without striving. I was settled to stay there the rest of my life. I had adapted and, during the next five years, learned to walk by the Spirit in ever-changing circumstances.

By 2010, I had surrendered in more ways than I could count. I was no longer striving with God or myself. I was living in grace, serving without compromise to God or comparison with others.

Core Scriptures:
John 6:66–69; Romans 8:5–11; Hebrews 12:12–17; Psalm 42;
Galatians 5:25

25

JOSEPH'S TWO YEARS

What happened to Joseph during those two full years in the dungeon? No one but God knows for sure. Whatever happened, after two years, Joseph was no longer praying for escape. Instead, he ended up advising Pharaoh on matters of state. Joseph had been transformed, becoming a partaker of the divine nature of God, no longer a prisoner of his fearful nature and the world's corruption.

That is what promises will do when they have fully taken over our lives. They leave us with no way out of our situation but no way to deny the word of God, either. We are in Him and He in us. The rest is just details.

When I asked, "Wouldn't you give anything to know what happened to Joseph during those last two years," now, in the spring of 2010, I was about to find out for myself.

When you keep a promise alive along with the expectation of a material outcome, then you are going to be forced to mortgage the promise with other promises (just as we might refinance our houses and include existing debts in the new mortgage). After a while, your debt (which is what a promise becomes when it moves from grace to works) becomes more than you can pay. The interest alone weighs you down and you collapse under the weight of impossibility.

For Joseph, he had to accept that the butler had forgotten him and was not going to send any help that would get him out of that prison. In that death of his soul life, Joseph had to decide if God had also forgotten him. If Joseph decided that God had not forgotten him, then he needed to understand why he was still in the dungeon.

"If your faith is not working, try forgiving," the Lord said to me one day. That shocked me. How could forgiveness make a difference in my receiving? Wasn't forgiveness letting go? Wasn't faith a way of taking hold?

Yes and no. Forgiveness is receiving new grace for today, letting go of the results of yesterday. Faith is letting go of control and our sense of entitlement that develops as we serve God as servants instead of children. So, forgiveness is letting go and receiving; faith is letting go and receiving—they are one. My faith in Jesus gives me forgiveness. His forgiveness gives me a new faith.

When the Lord said, "Try forgiving," God was after the debts that I had accumulated to myself, others and Himself.

Forgiveness releases. I had to release myself from outcome-based faith. I also needed to free myself from expectation. Joseph had a promise of rulership, but found himself a slave. He rose in rulership in Potiphar's house, but found himself a prisoner. He then rose in rulership in the prison, but found himself forgotten. Joseph was trying to salvage the dream but God was planning to resurrect Joseph. Still, Joseph, like all of us, was having a difficult time dying.

Forgiveness means to let something go, to send it out, to free it. Forgiveness has been extended to all of humanity but God is not into compelling us into liberty or salvation.

When something locks up in our life, we (not God or the devil) are the cause. If we believe that our circumstances must change in order for us to continue trusting and enjoying God, then that's a big red flag that we need to release our attachment to those circumstances. Joseph had to reconcile that the word of the Lord and His promises to him were true—even if *none* of God's promises came to pass before his eyes.

Joseph had to let go of his dream in order to enter into his destiny. He had to enter the presence behind the veil where there is no debt, condemnation or accusation; there is only grace and forgiveness. Total freedom!

Core Scriptures:
John 6:67–69; Galatians 3:1–14; Mark 11:22–26;
Matthew 18:21–35; Hebrews 6:19–20

26

DO NOT SEEK AN EXPLANATION; SEEK A NEW EXPERIENCE

During the next two years, I encountered the Lord in many ways. I met Him in the book of Job, with my myopic vision having shrunk down my world to questions of "Why me?" The Lord also took me to Habakkuk's questions where he asked God why the wicked prospered and why there was no justice.

In both stories of Habakkuk and Job, God's answers led to more questions. God *asked* Job, "Tell Me where I store the snow?" and "Were you there when I stretched out the heaven and gave stars their names?" To Habakkuk the Lord said, "You think it is crazy now—just wait and see what is coming—but know that the just shall live by his faith."

Similarly, God challenged me, along with my questions, by shining the light on how small my thinking had become. I thought again of Joseph; he had to let go of his dream of becoming a great ruler. I know he succeeded, because when his brothers finally came to Egypt, ten years later—to buy food and ended up bowing down to him—only then did he remember the dream.

He had let it go, but God hadn't.

I went to a writer's conference, where I ended up having it out with God. Way up in the hills of Northern California, I decided to do what Habakkuk had done.

> I will stand my watch and set myself on the rampart, and watch and see what He will say to me, and what I will answer when I am corrected. (Habakkuk 2:1)

I knew I would be corrected but that is often how you get to repentance—by rehearsing your sorrow, questioning God's justice and defending your actions. In faith, without doubting, just complaining, you pour out your heart to Him and wait for His response.

Meanwhile, back home at our Sunday morning service, Paul Cain was giving our congregation a prophetic word, "Don't seek an explanation for the past season but seek a new experience with God." Cammy told me over the phone what Paul Cain had said, knowing it was for me. I had spent the day in prayer and heard the same thing: "OK. I got it. Let it go and find the Lord anew."

There are so many stories of the Lord encountering me—demanding faith from me again without my demanding His finishing what I thought He had promised. What we think He said or meant doesn't matter as much as that He spoke. What we did, or didn't do, doesn't matter as much as we think, either.

I am sure Joseph had time to imagine so many different scenarios. "If only I had not bragged so much," or "If only I had stayed out of Potiphar's house during the day while my master was away." These should-have, could-have, and would-have thoughts leave us with a feeling of missed opportunity. However, God does not have a "plan

A" for us and then a "plan B" when we mess up. He only has plan Jesus.

Do we actually think that we catch the Father off guard when we make a stupid decision or when someone else takes advantage of us, ruining our future? The Father is trillions of decisions in front of our next decision and He follows us wherever we go. He cannot be out-smarted or outwitted. He will always win in His Son.

In the months that followed, after forgiving and letting go, I also repented for my selfish, proud thinking. I was still carrying grief and sorrow when I saw the Lord high and lifted up, in the fall of 2010, in London. I saw the glory of God.

There is nothing like the glory of God to wake you up to truth. Like Isaiah, I encountered the Lord and was undone. This time, it was not about my situation but my condition: "Woe is me for I am undone! Because I am a man of unclean lips, and I dwell in the midst of a people of unclean lips; for my eyes have seen the King, the Lord of hosts." (Isaiah 6:5)

My cry reached heaven and the angel brought the coal from the altar to cleanse my lips. It is wild to imagine kissing a burning coal but that is just what you do when you are undone. You will embrace anything that the Lord gives you to kiss.

Joseph might have had a moment like that. The Lord may have stepped into his woe, causing Joseph to cry out, "Woe is me." After Isaiah saw the Lord, became undone, cried out, and was cleansed, he heard a new sound. He heard the voice of the Lord saying, "Whom shall I send, and who will go for us?"

It was a new message, a new moment. It was the glory of God.

Core Scriptures:

Job 32–42; Habakkuk 1–3; 2 Corinthians 2:14; Isaiah 6:1–10

27

TIME TO GIVE IT ALL AWAY

In London, when I saw the Lord in His glory, it was a new experience for me in the Lord. I was undone, letting go of everything that I was holding. I could not wait to enter into the new. But what was it?

I returned to the United States, sensing the Lord calling Jubilee Church to do a conference called the "Awakening." I felt that now was the time to awaken love. As we prepared for the conference, Isaiah 6 continued to be a source of inspiration. Every day I would meditate on the experience Isaiah had with the Lord and was enjoying being undone, cleansed and called anew.

As we approached our conference, which was to take place in February 2011, we felt the Lord leading us to give away all that we had accumulated in our ministry life as a church. In twenty-seven years of ministry, we had learned much, done much and had many anointing and callings. I asked everyone, who wanted to give away what they had, to come and help.

All our ministers and ministries responded. They brought their experience and anointing to bless every guest coming to the conference. Soon, this revelation led us to give away all the teachings and materials we had produced over the years, even all the CDs and DVDs. The weeks leading up to the conference became really fun as we prepared to give away everything.

The conference came and we gave it all away. It felt like we were moving. The Sunday morning after the conference as I was preparing to recap the conference with the story of Jesus and the twelve baskets of loaves and fishes, I kept hearing the phrase "burnt offering." *Where was that coming from?* I thought to myself. The phrase kept returning, so I finally figured I had better look it up.

I went to my Bible and saw that burnt offering was a pleasing aroma to the Lord, first offered by Noah after he had successfully left the Ark a year after entering it. Noah offered one of every clean animal that he had brought into the Ark as a burnt offering. God had commanded Noah to bring seven clean animals for every two unclean animals that he gathered into the Ark. The offering touched God's heart:

> And the Lord smelled a soothing aroma. Then the Lord said in His heart, "I will never again curse the ground for man's sake, although the imagination of man's heart is evil from his youth; nor will I again destroy every living thing as I have done." (Genesis 8:21)

The Lord's acceptance of Noah's offering altered His heart and God declared a new future and hope for mankind.

Similarly, Abraham offered a burnt offering when he was asked to offer up Isaac. Remember just as Abraham was going to kill Isaac, the Lord called out to Abraham and intervened? That was when the ram caught in the thicket appeared and Abraham offered up the ram in place of Isaac. It was after this burnt offering of the ram that the Lord spoke a second time, declaring a new future, enlarging His promises over Abraham to include blessings and multiplication. He foretold that Abraham's seed would possess the gates of their enemies.

As I sat in my home reading those stories, I heard the Lord say, "Tell my people, because they have given away freely what they had gained of me, it is good. I now re-create their future."

This rocked my world because, first, He had received our offering, calling it a burnt offering—a sweet and soothing aroma—and, second, because of what was ahead of us, our re-created future.

God loves to re-create our future. He takes what has led us to this moment, using the very things that have brought us here and, when offered as a burnt offering, receives them in smoke—a sweet and smoothing aroma. Then, He frees our future again. A new experience with God is better than an explanation, and giving it all away opens a future wide and wonderful in God.

Core Scriptures:
Genesis 8:20–22; Genesis 22:8–19; Leviticus 1:9, 13, 17;
John 10:17–18; Hebrews 13:14–15

28

"SUDDENLIES" TAKE A LONG TIME

After the butler had been released, Joseph stayed in prison for two full years. While he sat there without natural hope, Joseph was being transformed from within. Something so wonderful was happening. He was no longer a "Hebrew stolen, betrayed and falsely imprisoned"; he was becoming free inside and no longer in need of deliverance. What Joseph did not know was that his "suddenly" was about to happen.

Pharaoh dreamed two dreams. Both left everyone dumbfounded. He saw seven fine-looking fat cows come out of the river followed by seven ugly and gaunt cows, who came out of the river and ate the fine-looking fat cows. The next dream was like the first but this time it was seven heads of grain that were plump and good, followed by seven heads of grain blighted by the east wind which devoured the seven plump, good heads of grain.

Now, none of Pharaoh's magicians or wise men could interpret the dreams. It was then that the chief butler remembered the man he had forgotten in prison. He told Pharaoh about a young Hebrew who had accurately interpreted both his and the baker's dreams.

> Then Pharaoh sent and called Joseph, and they brought him quickly out of the dungeon; and he shaved, changed his clothing, and came to Pharaoh. (Genesis 41:14)

It was after I had been called up into heaven in October 2011, and began to sit with Jesus on His throne, experiencing my own "suddenly," that I realized how radical a future Joseph had stepped into. Joseph went from an imprisoned Hebrew to an elite Egyptian. He interpreted Pharaoh's dreams and gave him this advice:

> "Now therefore, let Pharaoh select a discerning and wise man and set him over the land of Egypt." (Genesis 41:33)

Joseph went on to say that this wise man should appoint officers over the land to collect 20% of the produce during the seven plentiful years. Pharaoh accepted Joseph's advice and decided, since Joseph was the only man to interpret the dream to his satisfaction, that Joseph was the man for the job. So, Joseph changed his clothes a second time in one day, receiving from Pharaoh fine linen clothes, a signet ring, golden chain and Pharaoh's second chariot.

The shift that took place in Joseph's life might have been entirely unacceptable to his rigid thinking as a "Hebrew trying to get home." But Joseph could become new because he had left the past behind.

When he received from Pharaoh the daughter of the priest of On as his wife, it didn't throw him or God. His two sons—Manasseh, "For God has made me forget all my toil and all my father's house," and Ephraim, "For God has caused me to be fruitful in the land of my affliction"—served as a testimony of what had happened in Joseph's heart. The Lord made him forget and had made him fruitful.

I believe these kinds of promotions take huge promise and great dismantling. Flesh and blood cannot inherit God's kingdom. So when we try inheriting the kingdom with our efforts, we experience a journey similar to the one experienced by Joseph. We hold our integrity for as long as we can, honoring the word that was spoken until the cry of our heart becomes, "Get me out of here!"

Then there is an awful silence—as heaven moves in to reconcile us back through encounters similar to mine or Joseph's. We let go of our arguments, encounter the Lord in His glory and reconcile the past, forgetting what we've left behind.

It is true. My experience with the Lord in the presence behind the veil has so eclipsed the suffering I have had walking out His promise. When you can say freely, "Thank you for everything I have walked through, for I see the purpose of God was greater than the injustice of man," then you are free.

Core Scriptures:
Genesis 41; Romans 8:18; Colossians 3:1–4; Luke 24:25–26

29

DO NOT BE GRIEVED OR
ANGRY WITH YOURSELF

Joseph stepped into the authority Pharaoh gave him and succeeded. For seven years, he gathered 20% of the bountiful harvest into storehouses. Joseph had forgotten the journey of the past and embraced the change of the new. Prospering in the land of his affliction, Joseph lived his new life.

Then, one day, his brothers showed up.

There they were—all ten of them bowing down at Joseph's feet. (Benjamin, Joseph's youngest brother, had remained home with their father, Jacob.) Suddenly, in that moment, Joseph remembered his dream. *This is what God meant when I had those dreams twenty years ago,* Joseph thought to himself.

Then Joseph took his brothers through a series of experiences (that might seem cruel but were necessary for them to be able to receive him again). First, he accused them of being spies and locked them up in prison. "We are honest men," they implored Joseph.

In response, he offered them the chance to prove their honesty by sending one man back to their father's house to bring back Benjamin, their youngest brother. In prison, they began to speak together saying, "We are truly guilty concerning our brother, for we saw the anguish of his soul when he pleaded with us, and we would not hear; therefore this distress has come upon us." (Genesis 42:21)

Joseph, hearing their revelation, turned aside to weep for his brothers, who didn't know he understood their language because Joseph looked and spoke like an Egyptian. He sent them home but kept Simeon locked up until they brought Benjamin back to prove their innocence. When the nine brothers returned home without Simeon, they found the money they had used to purchase their grain returned to them in the sacks of grain. Jacob refused to part with Benjamin until, eventually, the famine forced him.

This story of discovery is an intricate drama, something that only God could orchestrate, and a man who held no bitterness or judgment could implement.

When the famine forced them to return to Egypt, Judah promised Jacob that Benjamin would be returned to him safely. Upon their arrival in Egypt, Joseph welcomed them to his home for a meal and Simeon was restored to them. The brothers found themselves seated in their birth order.

Sitting bewildered, they watched as Benjamin was favored by receiving a meal five times larger than anyone else. Their world was being dismantled as one uncanny thing after another happened but the clincher happened the next day. They left for home without knowing that their money was again in their sacks. Even more, Joseph had placed a silver cup in Benjamin's sack.

The eleven brothers had just left the city when Joseph's steward overtook them, accusing them of stealing Joseph's sliver cup. Denying this, they boasted again of their innocence saying, "With whomever of your servants it is found, let him die, and we also will be my lord's slaves." (Genesis 44:9)

Imagine their horror when the cup appeared in Benjamin's sack. Tearing their clothes, they returned to the city to accept their guilt. Joseph said they could all go free to their father's house in peace except the man "in whose hand the cup was found." Benjamin was now a slave!

Judah asked to approach Joseph. He shared the story of his father, his love for Benjamin and how his father had lost his other son (Joseph) years before. Judah explained that if he returned home without Benjamin, "I will bring down his gray hair with sorrow to the grave." Judah asked to be made Joseph's slave instead of Benjamin.

Twenty years before, Judah was the very brother who had decided to sell Joseph to the Ishmaelites, yet now he was pleading for Benjamin's life. At this, Joseph could no longer restrain himself. He commanded his servants to leave the room while he made himself known to his brothers.

Joseph collapsed into his humanity, weeping aloud, "I am Joseph; does my father still live?" His brothers stood dumbfounded and could not answer him, "For they were dismayed in his presence."

Now what was going to happen to them?

Core Scriptures:
Genesis 42:44; 37:1–11; 37:26–27

30

GOD AND HIS ETERNAL GOOD

J oseph called his brothers to his side.

"Please come near me." So they came near him. Then he said:

"I am Joseph your brother, whom you sold into Egypt. But now, do not therefore be grieved or angry with yourselves because you sold me here; for God sent me before you to preserve life.

For these two years the famine has been in the land, and there are still five years in which there will be neither plowing nor harvesting. And God sent me before you to preserve a posterity for you in the earth, and to save your lives by a great deliverance.

So now it was not you who sent me here, but God; and He has made me a father to Pharaoh, and lord of all his house, and a ruler throughout all the land of Egypt. Hurry and go up to my father and say to him, 'Thus says your son Joseph: God has made me lord of all Egypt; come down to me, do not tarry.'" (Genesis 45:4–9)

Joseph, a powerful man, declared it was God's will, not his brothers, that had brought him to Egypt. It was Joseph's letting go, forgetting his father's house, ruling in the midst of his enemies and prospering in the land of his affliction—all the result of those two years in his prison cell where he encountered God, where he reconciled himself back to God or, rather, as the Lord reconciled Joseph into his "recreated future."

Joseph's brothers only experienced a taste of what Joseph had been through but it was enough to make them understand that they could no longer conceal their betrayal from their father. Still this truth would bring joy and salvation to the entire household.

Can we do this something like this? Probably not. I know that I cannot on my own. However, when we experience the Lord in our trauma, find freedom to forget and the freedom to become fruitful in the very place we found ourselves bound and afflicted, then we can and will.

Joseph was not forcing himself to do the right thing because this was God's doing, not his. Joseph had only submitted to the Lord in the midst of the trauma, undoing the evil of its venom and reconciling himself and his brothers back to the Lord's goodness and faithfulness. Joseph had become a new person. Therefore, when the Lord called for it all to come full circle, Joseph moved with genuine humility and love for his betrayers.

Our betrayers are our gift from God to enter into death, so that the life of Christ may become manifest in our mortal bodies.

Joseph lived out the rest of his days in this freedom but his brothers could not fully enter into it. When Jacob died in Egypt years later and all twelve brothers had buried their father back in the land of Canaan, the ten brothers feared that Joseph might exact his revenge now that their father was gone. They sent Joseph a plea by messenger that they said came from their father: "I beg you, please forgive the trespass of your brothers and their sin; for they did evil to you. Now, please, forgive the trespass of the servants of the God of your father." (Genesis 50:17)

Joseph wept when he heard this. His brothers came, bowed and said, "Behold we are your servants." They had never received their forgiveness. They were still in the slavery of their sin and therefore tormented by fear. They were not free but slaves. What Joseph said to them must have overwhelmed them and hopefully took away their guilt and shame.

All of us will betray one another and cause each other to stumble, sometimes with animosity, other times in ignorance. But when we can submit to God in the midst of the trauma, we can enter into redemption's story, receive our recreated future and see our betrayers as instruments in the hand of our Father's eternal good.

Joseph comforted his brothers and opened their hearts again:

> Joseph said to them. "Do not be afraid, for am I in the place of God? But as for you, you meant evil against me; but God meant it for good, in order to bring it about as it is this day, to save many people alive. Now therefore, do not be afraid; I will provide for you and your little ones." And he comforted them and spoke kindly to them." (Genesis 50:19–21)

This is the power of redemption and the power of the transformation of the cross. Where our life is lost and His life is found. Where we have been conformed to His death and attained to His resurrection, where God's purposes are seen to save many people's lives.

Core Scriptures:

Genesis 45–50; Philippians 1:12–18; 2 Corinthians 1:3–4; 4:11

31

BEARING FRUIT OR HARVESTING FRUIT?

The holy hush of heaven invaded our sanctuary in the fall of 2011 while our conference speaker, Mike Becchio, shared with us. All of us together sat there for forty-five minutes in utter stillness—no one made a sound; no one got up to leave. As I sat in silence, the Lord spoke to me: "You have been good to abide in Me but you constantly leave and try to harvest what you see when you are abiding in Me. It's time to make a choice. Choose abiding or choose harvesting."

Wow. That was strong. I sat in silence, pondering these words.

The choice was obvious. Since my youth, I had been invited, wooed and beckoned by the Holy Spirit to seek His face. The Lord doesn't so much lead you to impossible decisions as He aids you in making the one that you have been making all along. Yes. We get distracted and even shipwrecked in our faith. We have more to do than we are able and our experiences leave us questioning our faith and ourselves.

But we were called to God long before we were born. Paul said in 2 Timothy that we are saved and called in Christ before the foundation of the world. So before time began, we were established in

Christ, in His salvation and calling. All that remains is for time to unfold and for Christ to be revealed in us.

So, in that morning conference service, I said, "Yes," again. "I choose You. I choose to abide."

The conference continued. A day later, the Lord said to me, "I want you to laugh every time something frustrates you or when you feel challenged to fix or solve or do. I want you to laugh." As worship began, I went into the sanctuary and a dancer ran in front of me. I thought she was out of order, a little too much...then I remembered to laugh.

So, I laughed and the presence of God began to flood my being. I laughed and laughed and laughed. I didn't realize it at the time but the Lord was shifting my responsibilities from earth to heaven, He was teaching me how to sit with Him on His throne.

He was very kind to show me in Psalm 2: "He who sits in heaven shall laugh..." But more than just laugh, the Lord sets His Son in Zion. He gives Him an inheritance of nations and the rulership of a rod of iron. This is Jesus, of course! But I am *in* Christ and I am sitting *with* Christ.

For the next three weeks, I found myself disconnecting from earthly concerns and connecting to the eternal finished work of Christ. I danced a lot and laughed a lot. Suddenly all my efforts, which had once seemed so important, and all the stuff that had frustrated me no longer mattered. Unlike other encounters with God, the difference this time was that I had moved into a new place. I was not just visiting.

Revelation is looking through a window. Transfiguration is being changed into the image of what you see there. Through revelation, I had seen all of God's wonderful creations. I had seen the Christ but refuted His call to the cross. I had seen and heard the words of eternal life and struggled with where they led.

Now I sat with the Lord, laughing and singing, so grateful for everything that had happened in my life. The Lord said, "Don't tell anyone what I have done for you, nor teach about it. I simply want you to learn to live from here and teach from here. What you teach doesn't matter for now." Sure. I was OK with that. When asked what was going on, I didn't want to lose this place of grace. So I would say, "The Lord gave me a promotion."

God had received my decision to abide—which was a decision I had made many times throughout my life. However, this time, my address and job description changed. I was to come and sit with Christ, to offer the "fat and the blood." (The fat is our praise. The blood is His redemption.) Instead of thinking and praying about how to engage the work of the Lord from earth, I would now go to heaven (not in my body but in my spirit) and sit in the presence of my Father. There we would laugh and play in His finished, glorious, and wonderful work!

Core Scriptures:
John 15:1–6; Psalm 27:8; 2 Timothy 1:8–10; Psalm 2; Ezekiel 44:5

32

WHEN GOD CALLED ME UP

When the Lord called me up to sit with Him in heavenly places, my mouth was filled with laughter, literally. I would laugh and laugh all day because I was seeing everything from a different perspective—heaven's perspective.

In heaven, Jesus is supreme. His death and resurrection are complete. Nothing is missing. In fact, Heaven is abuzz about what the Lord has done. He has made everyone who believes in Jesus Christ justified and glorified. It is overwhelming, to say the least, but also wonderful. Joy is the atmosphere. Faith is the reality. Hope is as brilliant as a newborn child, just greater, and it even increases over time. It doesn't diminish as it does here on earth.

In that heavenly place, I had to let go of a lot of things to get up into my Father's lap. Among the first, I had to learn to forgive debts – even those debts (ones that were *delayed* promises) that I had refinanced into *mortgaged* promises. I had to disengage from trying to make everything once promised into a reality seen and experienced in the present. Attempting to do so, I was most miserable, but we are told by Paul that, "If in this life only we have hope in Christ, we are of all men the most pitiable." (1 Corinthians 15:19)

Imagine trying to bring all of heaven into the earth and basing your success on how many promises you saw fulfilled. In my case, the promises had far exceeded my experiences on earth. Now there were more unfulfilled promises in my life than I could remember. Even Abraham could not bring to pass all the promises made to him in his lifetime!

When you let go of your right to fulfillment, you open the door to the Lord's fulfillment in His eternal purposes (which are always far greater than what you first realized).

Shortly after the Lord had called me up to sit with Him in heavenly places, I revisited the promises He had made back in 1999, specifically those describing the revival and His reign. I went there in the Spirit, having entered the holiest by the blood of Jesus, through the new and living way He had consecrated through His flesh. I praised the Lord in that place and adored His work.

To be accepted and received based on what Christ had done alone and, to have such intimate access to the Father sitting on the throne of grace, was overwhelming. I wanted to thank and praise Him. (It is actually my job now, but I will explain that later.) This entrance into God is recorded in Hebrews 10:19–23. It is real.

In Hebrews 10:23, we are told: "Let us hold fast our confession of our hope without wavering, for He who promised is faithful." So many times in the past, I had done this very thing when I was trying to bring the promises to pass here on earth. I filled the sanctuary with scriptures, memorizing whole chapters and verses, but it had led to nothing.

But, now, as I sat in the heavens laughing, the thought came to me. "Bring the confession of hope to the Father as an offering of praise." So, I did and was blown away. Nothing could have prepared me for what I was about to experience. First, the promises had grown. They were vibrantly alive, even living inside the words I had memorized or been given.

Since the word of God is eternal, I guess that shouldn't seem strange. Even when heaven and earth pass away, His words will remain. But I had always felt that the promises were alive while I believed and that they were alive to the level I could experience them *here on earth*.

What I experienced in heaven was that all of the promises had instead multiplied; the seed had fallen into the ground, died and multiplied.

Core Scriptures:
Psalm 126:1–2; Romans 8:28–30; Acts 7:5; John 8:56;
Hebrews 4:1–10; Isaiah 49:21

33

THE HIGHWAY OF HOLINESS

The first promise I brought to the Father as an offering of praise was Isaiah 35.

Before this encounter with the Lord, I had memorized this entire chapter, meticulously going over each verse until I had committed the whole chapter to memory. This book of Isaiah contains the hallmark verse of the coming of the Lord, and I filled the air with it until the Lord said, "Let it fall into the ground and die." Well, it had died, all right. Suddenly, I no longer knew the verses by heart.

Now, in this heavenly place, when I brought up this chapter, not verse by verse but the essence of it before the Lord, it was as though I had stepped into a special place. I *saw* the word; I saw hills alive with flowers, the lame leaping, dancing and singing, water everywhere...even the highway of holiness! *Why can I see this?* I wondered. In fact, I didn't just see it—I was feeling, experiencing and living in it.

I heard the Father say, "These promises are yours. They were given to you. We will meet here and here we will dwell." The beauty of the Lord was all around. Joy filled the atmosphere and laughter filled my mouth. It was as though I was in a dream. I began bringing forward all the words I had heard, but not in haste, because it takes time to dwell inside of His word. Before I would memorize His word, process the meaning and even see its conclusion or promise—all steps important for digestion. Now, I was partaking of the *divine nature* of the promise. I was enjoying God. I was breathing, drinking, eating and living the word.

So, in that place, I brought forward Isaiah 60 and its essence flooded my being. Even when walking alone, without a Bible, I was inside the word. (I had memorized Isaiah 60 before but could no longer remember the verses verbatim.)

Instead, I was living in the promise of Isaiah 60. Glory shone all around. Rising up, I saw the abundance of the sea, children and the restoration of worship. I saw offerings to the Lord brought from every corner of the world as His worship was restored. Gates opened continually, bringing in the wealth of nations. I was walking in the word. Like Abraham of old, I was walking through the Promised Land.

When we bring to the Father His word as our confession of hope, His pleasure is immense. To delight in acknowledging His faithfulness is amazing. He would rejoice with me, in my discoveries, pointing me toward new meanings, feelings and truths. I would hear, see and know things I had never known before.

Isaiah 60 became one word: restoration, and the goal of worship. I love this chapter now. I don't have to do anything to bring it to pass. I get to live *in it* as though it has already happened. I get to live in the presence behind the veil with Him who gives life to the dead and calls life into being. I understand now that everything in heaven encourages us to live as though the promise has been completed. Even the highway of holiness prophesied in Isaiah 35 is a real highway where the ransomed of the Lord return with singing, joy and laughter in their mouths and where sorrow and sighing fly away.

There is no limit to the power of His promise in His presence. I would look forward to this time every day when I visited with my Father in His word. There, I experienced His word as finished, enjoying the truth and letting the eternal decide my moment.

For five months, the Father would not let me explain any of this. His only command was, "Learn to live here and minster from here."

Core Scriptures:
Isaiah 35; Psalm 126; 2 Peter 1:2–4; Isaiah 60; Romans 4:17

34

I A GOT PROMOTION

For five months, I could only explain my confusing behavior by telling people, with a laugh, that "I had gotten a promotion."

The Lord had called me to sit with Him in heavenly places. I didn't try to explain this place or what happened to me. I just enjoyed it. Every day, I couldn't wait to be with the Lord. I treasured my time alone with Him, unfettered and unchallenged. I would praise, laugh, sing and laugh some more. The blood of the Lamb purged my conscience and the water of His word washed my body clean. Visiting my confession of hope and living in His word was wonderful.

At church, I would sit in my office and laugh. At first, I wondered what people would think but I was comforted when Joan Bach, our office manager at the time, said, "We love hearing your laughter. It brings the peace of God as well as faith and strength." *Good*, I thought, because everything was making me laugh.

Even more, during worship services, I was compelled to dance (which was a little embarrassing). No one made me but I was like David, joyously dancing, "at play" before the Lord, and the coming of His Ark into Jerusalem.

I have always been an expressive worshipper. I even have had some dances named after me, one in particular, called "the monkey dance." It is a simple dance the Lord taught me in 2001 when I was in the prison season with Joseph, trying to hold the promises alive. I was taking out the trash one evening, fighting heaviness, when I heard the voice of the Lord say, "Do the monkey dance."

I wondered, *What's the monkey dance?* The Lord was so kind. He simply said, "Put down your trash can and flail your limbs wildly with all your might." I thought, *I can do that.* So I put down my trash can and flailed my arms and legs wildly while jumping all around. You know, I felt great. The heaviness vanished and I was free.

The next Sunday, I shared the experience with the congregation. When I got to the monkey dance part, I asked if they would like to see it. Of course, they said, "Yes!" Who doesn't want to see a grown man make a fool of himself? I said, "OK. I will show you if you promise to do it, too." I had them now, their curiosity getting the best of them. So, I did the monkey dance. Then they did the monkey dance and the rest is history.

Several months went by and I received an invitation to visit a church in Hong Kong. When I arrived, the pastor took me to lunch at the top of a gigantic skyscraper. While we sat eating sushi, the pastor asked me to teach his congregation the monkey dance! He had been to our church the Sunday that Jubilee did the monkey dance and now he wanted me to share the dance with his evangelical congregation. "I have been brought to Hong Kong because of the monkey dance," I told Cammy that night when I called home.

Once, the monkey dance brought me freedom. Now it is my happy dance, because I am free. The same arms and legs move everywhere but, because of the freedom I am experiencing, they move in joy and celebration. I do not dance to become happy or persuade others to enter worship. I am just exploding on the inside because of all the joy I am experiencing sitting with Jesus.

During those five months, I had to explain to guest speakers, "I am going to go up to the front and dance. Something has happened to me and I must express my praise." Everyone was gracious. Still I couldn't tell anyone what had happened except Cammy, of course, and a few of the staff.

Often, I sat in my office laughing, rejoicing in the worship and being free. Everything seemed so funny: our human efforts to accomplish the Lord's work, our anger over the sins in the world. All the hustle and bustle and striving and strife; it seemed so funny. I found myself saying, again and again, "Everything is important and nothing is important. Everything matters and nothing matters."

This was the truth of my experience with God—which all started the day I got frustrated with someone dancing in front of me.

Core Scriptures:
Hebrews 10:18–23; 2 Samuel 6:14–23

35

THE PLAYFULNESS OF GOD

D id you know that laugher in heaven is the playfulness of God? Yes. It is the Lord laughing at His enemies because He sees their day is coming. God laughs with us as we enter into His pleasure. David knew this when he wrote in Psalm 16:11, "In Your presence is fullness of joy; at Your right hand are pleasures forevermore."

During those five months, I was laughing, dancing and enjoying God, drunk like the disciples on the day of Pentecost. It didn't matter if I was sitting in my office, doing chores at home, walking or working, I was enjoying God. Now, the Lord really helped me whenever I questioned the irresponsibility of such behavior. I did a study on the Hebrew word, "laughing," and found it to mean "to laugh in pleasure or distraction by implication to play."

When David came home to bless his household after successfully bringing the Ark of the Covenant into the tabernacle he had set up in Jerusalem, his wife, Michal, met him with scorn. She said:

"How glorious was the king of Israel today, uncovering himself today in the eyes of the maids of his servants, as one of the base fellows shamelessly uncovers himself!"

> So David said to Michal, "It was before the Lord, who chose me instead of your father and all his house, to appoint me ruler over the people of the Lord, over Israel. Therefore I will play *music* before the Lord. And I will be even more undignified than this, and will be humble in my own sight. But as for the maidservants of whom you have spoken, by them I will be held in honor." (2 Samuel 6:20b–2)

I added italics to the word, "music" because that's how the word appears in my Bible and it helps make sense of the word, "play." It might be hard to see that David is actually saying, "I will play before the Lord" but he was. David was playing or laughing (because the word in Hebrew is the same) but "Michal, Saul's daughter looked through a window and saw King David leaping and whirling before the Lord, and she despised him in her heart." (2 Samuel 6:16) Imagine how that offended a playful God who enjoys interacting with His children in uninhibited worship and play.

This understanding of "play" helped me greatly because I was now one of those dancers in the front, offending people's sensibilities. I was playing before the Lord.

In March of 2012, five months after being called up into this experience, I was in England with our good friends, Rod and Julie Anderson, who pastor the Commonwealth Church in London. During worship, I found myself laughing and laughing. And, while dancing, I suddenly stopped and knelt down. I saw the Lord rolling around on a grassy hill with me! It was all I could do not to follow Him and roll on the floor.

I had become a holy roller (or at least I now understand how these manifestations took place). You are in the Spirit, experiencing His presence, and God's playfulness begins to tickle you into a childlike display of selfless love. Without thinking about yourself, your problems or what it might look like to others, you celebrate, rejoicing and playing before the Lord.

In all these things, I have found the Lord to be fully confident in the work of the cross. He is in victory and joy. Yes, I am aware that all is not right in the earth, but it is in heaven. The Lord never misses a beat.

Two weeks before my trip to London, God released me to share my experience of heaven. So at the Commonwealth Church, I told everyone what I had seen—that there was a place to live on the other side of the cross, a place that had been prepared for us by Jesus. I told them it was a place of habitation, rest and joy. That Sunday morning, the entire church walked through the cross (literally) and entered purposefully into the place prepared for them. For some, I am sure it was a visit, a revelation and an isolated experience. For others, who knows? Maybe God invited them to stay and reside with Him.

Core Scriptures:
Psalm 59:8; 16:11; 2 Samuel 6:14–23; Matthew 18:3; 21:15–16

36

DAVID WANTED TO BUILD GOD A HOUSE

David prospered after he brought the Ark to Jerusalem. Soon afterward, he lived in a nice house made of cedar. However, David wanted to build God a house. He told Nathan, the prophet, about what he wanted to do. Nathan said, "Go, do all that is in your heart, for the Lord is with you." (2 Samuel 7:3)

That night, the Lord spoke to Nathan with a message for David. God had never asked David to build Him a house (though David's son, Solomon, would be allowed to do so). Instead, the Lord said to David, "Your house and your kingdom shall be established forever before Me. Your throne shall be established forever." (2 Samuel 7:16)

David sat before the Lord and accepted His promise. There, David worshipped and rehearsed what Nathan had told him. Although David had intended to bless God by building Him a house, God had blessed him with a future and a hope.

This is so often the way of God when we seek to serve Him. He denies one request and gives us a better hope. Accepting this, and worshipping in this better hope, is hard if we have set our heart on doing. David would write many psalms about the Lord's temple and at the end of his life, would give Solomon the plans he had received from the Spirit for its construction.

David had sat before the Lord, worshipped Him and entered the Lord's gates with thanksgiving and His courts with praise, writing "One thing have I desired of the Lord, that will I seek: That I may dwell in the house of the Lord all the days of my life, to behold the beauty of the Lord, and to inquire in His temple." (Psalm 27:4) David did not let the natural "no" stop his spiritual progress.

He dwelt in the temple in heaven, fellowshipping with God in His sanctuary. David saw help come from the sanctuary and even God's procession into it. God's denial of David's request to build an earthly temple enabled David to enter fully into the Spirit of the temple that would be built.

When David gave Solomon the plans for the temple, they addressed more than architectural structures. They also described the divisions of priests as well as the provision of gold, silver and every article of worship. There was nothing missing. David had spent long hours before the Lord receiving these plans by His Spirit:

> Then David gave his son Solomon the plan for the vestibule, its houses, its treasuries, its upper chambers, its inner chambers, and the place of the mercy seat; and the plans for all that he had by the Spirit, of the courts of the House of the Lord, of all the chambers all around, of the treasuries of the house of God, and of the treasuries for the dedicated things; also for the division of the priests and the Levites, for all the work of the service of the house of the Lord, and for all the articles of service in the house of the Lord.

"All this," said David, "the Lord made me understand in writing, by His hand upon me, all the works of these plans." (1 Chronicles 28:11–13, 19)

When the Lord denies the action in the natural realm, He opens a door in the Spirit.

Even if David had not been a man of war who had spilled much blood, David could not have built the temple when he desired to do it (something he didn't understand until later). Rather, he would need to walk out failure, sin, forgiveness, recovery, confusion and even the census of Israel that brought judgment on the nation. David would have to worship at His footstool, sing, meditate, write and enjoy God – because, in David's discovery of the Lord, he was also growing in his capacity to see the Lord.

After the census, when David saw the angel with his sword drawn to destroy Jerusalem, he went up and purchased the threshing floor from Ornan, the Jebusite, for six hundred shekels of gold. Now David knew where to build the temple. Right where God met him.

Core Scriptures:
2 Samuel 7; 2 Chronicles 28; Psalm 27:4–6; 20:1–2; 68;
2 Chronicles 21, 22

37

THE DELIGHTFULNESS OF THE LORD

D avid never built the temple but he enjoyed it. He saw and even wrote up the plans for it. He imagined all its furnishings, treasuries, functions and priests—the Levites and their ministry. He saw everything by the Spirit.

We can, too. We can enter into the presence behind the veil. Entering into the confession of hope without wavering, we can stand in the presence of Him Whom we believe. We can receive life and hear and see what does not yet exist. God calls things that do not exist (here) as though they did, because they do in His presence (in the unseen) before they are seen. In God's presence, we can enjoy these things now, even though they are not yet here on earth.

We say, "I want to build you a house, God." He says, "I want to build you a house, Son." We enter into this opportunity to receive His word, love and faithfulness by fellowshipping with Him in His word. If we are not frantic to get a result or trying to force an outcome, we will be surprised at the level of discovery available to us.

Once I had walked through "the last two years of Joseph," as I called them, I was free to enter into the city that God had prepared for me. In this, I had to let go and discover the Lord again, free of the debts of unfulfilled promise, missed moments and all my other disappointments. Like Joseph, I had to let that go so I could be called up by the King and receive a new assignment, one that I couldn't have fathomed or embraced in the beginning.

David delighted himself in the Lord, even seeing the Lord in His temple:

> One thing I have desired of the Lord, that will I seek; that I may dwell in the house of the Lord all the days of my life, to behold the beauty of the Lord, and to inquire in His temple.
>
> For in the time of trouble He shall hide me in His pavilion; in the secret place of His tabernacle He shall hide me; He shall set me high upon a rock.
>
> And now my head shall be lifted up above my enemies all around me; Therefore I will offer sacrifices of joy in His tabernacle; I will sing, yes, I will sing praises to the Lord. (Psalm 27:4–6)

David beheld the beauty of the Lord (which means delightfulness of the Lord). In that place of great delight, David could inquire in His temple. There, he found victory and a place of safety. Lifted up above his enemies, David could offer up sacrifices of joy and sing—yes, sing.

Because I had primarily focused on the material (worldly fulfillment), I had become locked up in the limitations of this life. But David was different. He saw the resurrection of Jesus, a temple in heaven from where he received his writings and plans. David entered into victories untold and, even when driven from his home by Absalom, he told the priest to leave the Ark in Jerusalem. His faith was in the invisible God and the unseen sanctuary. David saw the Lord high and lifted up. He knew the Lord would come and save him. His help was in the name of the Lord.

I no longer try to put uranium into clay pots, meaning: my seeking to stuff the glory of God into this earthly space. Why should I, when I can enter into the glory of the Lord now, passing out of time and space into eternity—into the place He has prepared for me?

The glory of the Lord follows me into my daily routines. The goodness of God invades my life from the inside out. There, in His presence, doing chores, during worship, prayer or study—while cleaning bathrooms or taking walks—the presence of the Lord is my sanctuary, His promises my delight, His faithfulness my boast.

Core Scriptures:
1 Chronicles 28:11–19; Hebrews 6:19–20; 10:19–22;
Romans 4:17; Psalm 27:4–6

38

THE HOUSE JESUS BUILT

J esus has built Himself a house and we are it! He went to prepare a place for us, through His death, burial and resurrection. In so doing, we became the dwelling place of God in the Spirit. God's promises are given to us and watched over, though not necessarily fulfilled in this life.

Still, we enjoy fellowship and faith in the many mansions in our Father's house that Jesus spoke of in John 14. When we watch His word, the Father loves us and He and Jesus, by the Spirit, make their home with us. Again, we are His house.

When I began to fellowship again with the Lord in His promises to me, I came alive and I mean *so* alive. We are no more able to build God a house than David was but, when we become God's house, we can see what we could not see before and enjoy what we could not enjoy.

The spoken word brings faith, hope and love. When it comes, there is excitement and anticipation. *It's going to happen and now,* I would always think but God is eternal and does not do time well—though He is the most longsuffering. He gives us the gift of time in order to inhabit eternity through the word spoken to us. Spoken eternity is living hope and promises; they are the house that Jesus built.

We are His house. He spoke His word to us but we don't have to accomplish it to possess it. We just need to hold fast to the rejoicing and confidence of hope to the end. In the Spirit, we enter into the promises of God as living, framing and holding the world together. We sit with Him in these heavenly places and enjoy God in His faithfulness. The outcome of our faith is the salvation of our souls as we love not our lives to the death.

I wish I could have always lived in the confidence and rejoicing of hope, but for a long time I could not hear, "No," "Not now," or anything like that. I had too much materialistic thinking and fear. Of course, I knew the Lord was faithful and His word true but I was trying to accomplish everything here and now. I was a desperate man whose identity had become what I could see and produce, though I lived with promises that I could not make visible.

I had to experience great grief at the loss of promises and hope, which I found were not lost at all. They are simply in heaven, where Christ is seated at the right hand of God. What I lost was my interpretation, dreams, desires, and wrong beliefs that things must turn right here to be right.

God is so great that He speaks with all confidence in imparting His divine nature through His promises; even as our soul life ebbs away, He is confident in Himself, His promises and His ability to perform them. How many of us have lost our childlike wonder of the Lord because of something that has failed to happen in the way we expected? I know I did.

We become free when we let go of our need to see our promises fulfilled before we can enjoy the reward. God rewards our faith, not our performance.

Even very temporal and immediate needs, such as health and wealth, can be enjoyed and should be enjoyed in the Spirit before they are seen in the natural world. When I enter the presence behind the veil and fellowship in the confession of my hope, I am not denying faith but activating it, for we walk by faith and not by sight. Trying to get faith into sight will not hasten its appearance but it will often frustrate grace.

Core Scriptures:
Hebrews 3:6; John 14:2–3; Ephesians 2:22; Hebrews 4:12; 11:3;
1 Peter 1:3–5

39

REVELATION IS WATCHING A MOVIE; TRANSFIGURATION IS THE MOVIE

Revelation, oh the wonder of revelation!

Knowledge is revealed by our Father. Rather than being obtained through our senses, abilities, capabilities, cognitive reasoning, works of law or adherence to the commandments, revelation is a gift. It is an invitation to come run with Him even though we don't understand, nor can we rightly interpret what He means when He said what He said, or showed us what He showed us.

In fact, we get it wrong, really wrong. We tire, become discouraged, make mistakes, fail, lose and get lost but our Lord doesn't. He is the author and the finisher of our faith. Jesus kept the joy before Him, despising the shame He endured on the cross and now He sits at the right hand of the Father.

We sit with Him, too. We do!

Revelation is looking through a window or into a mirror. Through the continual beholding of the glory of God in the face of Jesus, we become changed, transformed and transfigured into that glory. That is the way it works and why there is such warfare over our souls.

The warfare is to prevent you from beholding the glory of God in the face of Jesus. The struggle is to stop the seed in you from maturing by making you reject or refuse it, to become distracted by this life or overwhelmed in your suffering. The warfare is to stop you from looking through that window of revelation and to keep you from entering through the door, who is Jesus.

But the seed (promise) is eternal, incorruptible and does not fade away. Its design is in heaven. When conceived in us, we begin to partake of God's divine nature. The highest goal of a promise is to make you like Jesus and to make you a partaker of His divine nature. The other stuff is easy but transformation is God's finest work.

First, we looked like Adam. We were made of dust, natural, a living soul with our identity and life in this world. When we received Jesus, a transformation began. The seed took root, our spirit was reborn and our righteousness imputed. Still, we struggled with this imputed righteousness, trying to prove ourselves to be the sons and daughters of God. These efforts only masked our fears, unbelief, fleshly temptations and many other things we brought into our union with Christ. Yet, it doesn't matter. God won and you are His; His nature will prevail. You will die and He will live. The second Adam, Jesus Christ, will become the image that you, a life-giving spirit, will bear.

What is transformation? It is the glory of God turned inside out. It is the nature of God becoming our life. It will even affect our bodies as it did Jesus when He was transfigured on the Mount of Transfiguration or when Peter's shadow healed people. (It was not the shadow of the sun against Peter's natural body but the overshadowing of the glory from his inner man.) As Paul has said,

> Therefore we do not lose heart. Even though our outward man is perishing, yet the inward man is being renewed day by day. For our light affliction, which is but for a moment, is working for us a far more exceeding and eternal weight of glory, while we do not look at the things which are seen, but the things which are not seen. For the things which are seen are temporary, but the things which are not seen are eternal. (2 Corinthians 4:16–18)

Paul understood that clay pots leak and eventually perish. Still, in those pots, eternal glory is being deposited into our inner man to carry the Lord by the Spirit. We are being turned inside out!

That's why when I entered into God's presence and fellowshipped in the joy and laughter of heaven, my entire outlook changed. I was being changed from glory to glory through the Spirit. Although I was born in the image of the first Adam, so I will bear the image of the last Adam, Jesus Christ. His promises, His nods of grace and His go-aheads, these are the seeds of His image.

Core Scriptures:
Matthew 16:17–19; Hebrews 12:1–2; 2 Corinthians 4:6; 16–18; 1 Corinthians 15:45–49; Matthew 17:1–9

40

FRIEND OF GOD

Wat has most blown me away in this place that Jesus prepared for me and the Father called me to sit with Christ in, is the friendship that He has extended and valued. I love sitting with the Father in the Spirit, listening to His heart of love, kindness, and longsuffering toward us. I am in no hurry to move away from that fellowship and intimacy. I could sit forever in this never-ending supply of delightfulness in God.

And guess what? He delights in us with the same joy as we delight in Him. Friends know things that subordinates don't. Friends have access no servant enjoys. A servant might be valuable for what he or she does but a friend is valuable for who he or she is.

Sitting with God, I realize how often I did not understand the value He placed on friendship. I thought God's promises to me were outcome-driven, meant to change life on earth. Even when the Lord shared with me, in 1980, that the secret (or mystery) of my life was in 2 Peter 1:2–4, in "partaking in the divine nature," I couldn't appreciate this partaking as an end to itself.

We need to do something, produce something and accomplish something! You see, I was much more of a servant at heart, than a friend. Even though I heard the voice of God beckon me, followed His nods and heard His promises, I was still a servant in my heart, not a friend. Now, a servant is valuable for what he produces but he does not abide in the house forever. As a servant, you are temporary and that is a bit unsettling. Furthermore, unlike a friend, a servant doesn't know what His master is doing.

So, being a servant in my heart, when the Father shared His heart through revelation to me, I would think that He was doing this so that I could perform it. Imagine the frustration I caused my Father (that so many of us have caused Him) by always trying to produce, do and accomplish the word of God.

We run around as though what Jesus accomplished on the cross is not enough. We act as though God forgot something or that He needs us to complete His word so He can finish what He began. With a servant heart, it can get so bad that we fear that the Lord has changed His mind or disposition toward us.

Even more, that He is angry and will punish us for not doing what we were supposed to do. Seeing the Father that way is so servile and fearful but it was my attitude. Because I was a doer, I ran and ran and ran for a long time before I realized that the Father accepted me and desired my fellowship.

God makes promises so that His seed will be in me. In the course of our time together, walking in His promises and fellowshipping in His presence, I partake of His nature and we become one. True, the accomplishment of the word is important but secondary, since that only requires power on God's part, but our transformation needs time, beholding and the rest of faith.

I was a worker but God wanted a son. I was a doer but God wanted to share His nature, not His acts. He wanted me to know His ways, not His works. Small wonder I was frustrated all the time. I saw things that were wonderful but I couldn't bring them to pass. I had heard the Lord speak of His ways and understood His coming but I couldn't manufacture either on earth. Having a German heritage (my earthly father was German) with a bent towards industriousness, I wanted to do something, despite hearing the Father speak differently over me.

The voice of God is our calling in life. What we hear determines who we are. All of us are called to be children of God, given the intimate words to call Him, "Abba Father" from the Holy Spirit at our new birth. His promises are the seeds of our identity, transformation and our partaking of His divine nature. Friendship comes when value is placed on the One speaking, not just on what is being said.

Core Scriptures:
John 15:15; Galatians 3:1-9; Ephesians 1:5–6; Psalm 103:7;
Matthew 3:17; Romans 8:15

41

THE NOD OF GOD

Immediately in the new birth, the Holy Spirit begins speaking something new, something so wonderful, "Abba Father." Like a proud parent cooing to His child, "I am your daddy," the Holy Spirit imprints our spirits with these same words, "I am your Daddy."

But we are disciples, who move from children who know the Father to young men who are strong (because the word of God abides in us), overcoming the evil one. We pick up the promises of God, those nods, because He gives us invitation to do so. It is not like, "You have permission to pick that promise up," but more "Hey, why don't you believe that? This is for you. I am giving this promise to you."

The nod of God is the still, small voice inside, warm and inviting like the Abba Father is inside. So we often think, "I wish I could have that. I really want to know this. I feel like this is for me. This is speaking right to me." Those are the nod of God. They are subtle whispers that become the word of God abiding in us. They become our victory over the devil.

What part of God is most intriguing to you? What about God, above anything else, would you want to know and experience? Where are you drawn to when you enter into His presence in worship? Have you ever felt the whisper, the nod of God? You may say "no," but you have.

It is in sonship, not discipleship, that we understand the Lord's voice to us.

We must all grow strong in the word of God, unashamed and rightly dividing it. We must meditate and memorize scripture, learn doctrine and be able to give an answer to the hope that lies within us. We must know we are forgiven in the word, made righteous, sanctified and made holy. Yet all of this is our citizenship, not sonship.

Sonship is back to the Abba Father and God's nod to you. The nods of God are given in desire. They match your calling and identity. You want this and wish you could be so lucky. Someone else might think, *I would never want to be or do that.* Still, what you are thinking is, *I want that but I am afraid I will not be allowed or qualified.* That is desire cloaked in fear; feelings of servitude leaked into our identity as children.

I wanted to seek His face, not His hand. I said, "Your face will I seek." I wanted to walk as Moses, knowing God's ways, not His works. I wanted to see His glory and, yes, "If your presence does not go with us, I don't want to go on." But my fearful servant heart said, "That's all well and good but we need to move on. We have work to do."

God's nods come often in the stillness and quiet of God because, in stillness, we hear what our fearful, striving self cannot. We hear love, "Go ahead. Pick that up. It is for you." Trembling, we venture to pick up that promise that seems so great, so beyond us. It feels right. "That's me, but it couldn't be me, could it?"

The more time we spend in His presence, the more convincing the promise becomes because He gives life to the dead and calls those things that do not exist as though they did. God tells us, "Yes. That is yours and the longer you stay here, the more you know it."

Since my journey as a young man demanded that I spend time in His presence and word to overcome the evil one, I found the Lord nodding for me to pick up many wonderful truths. Every time I came to Him, there they were. But when I left God's presence to bring change into the world, the truths all went away.

I was confused and thought I must have been wrong or that I didn't do something right and had better read the directions again. I was acting like a servant, following the hear-do mentality. I was not acting like a son who should sit and see.

Maybe you've done the same thing; you have heard the voice of God, His nods, whispers, and love—Abba Father—and in your attempt to prove it, you lose it.

Core Scriptures:
Romans 8:15-17; I John 2:14; Timothy 2:15; Psalm 27:8; Exodus 33:14

42

YOU WERE MADE FOR THIS

"Why are you here?" Scrooge demanded of the Ghost of Christmas Past in the story, The Christmas Carol. The ghost replied, "For your reclamation." To be reclaimed is to be brought back to what we were made for; we are recovered, reclaimed, and redeemed.

Scrooge was not made to be a miserable miser. Instead, he was made to be a generous patriarch. His upbringing, fears, and choices had warped his identity. Only through a radical revelation of past, present and future could he repent. I love that story. It is the essence of redemption in Christ, the goal of transformation and why we are given such precious promises—to become who we were made to be.

But we have a war going on, of which I did not know the extent.

From the time God brought me out of my captivity into His glorious liberty, I have enjoyed deep fellowship and friendship with Him. In the past I had seasons of rich fellowship, but my soul warred against me. My fears and the strivings circumvented the gifts and pleasures of His presence and identity.

In heaven, our identity and worth are never in question. The Father receives us as His sons and daughters, welcoming us to join Him in

His promises and presence. Hope fills heaven more than anything and there is such a sense of playful possibility.

In His presence is the perpetual expectation of unveiling mercy and love, limitless boundless possibilities of the redemption in the Son. Literally, there is no scenario on earth that can stump heaven. Heaven is ablaze with redemption—all things have become new again and again.

In the past, I would leave this environment fully awakened to revelation and redemption. I would be like a kid with too many movies to watch and they were all so good. Heaven is like a mysterious place where you are fully known in the Son, loved by the Father and watched over by the Holy Spirit. Heaven is His presence and is our home, our city, and the builder and maker is God.

So when we enter into the presence behind the veil, we enter into heaven. It is similar to the way we enter our country's embassy in a foreign country. The problem is that when you leave the embassy, you're back in the foreign country.

Do you remember Lucy, who traveled with her sister and brothers to Narnia, through the wardrobe? There they grew, experienced life and became mighty kings and queens, until one day they stumbled back through the wardrobe and found that just a few moments had passed.

Eternity is the same way. In eternity, present and future coexist because they are no longer separated in time. Change can happen in a moment but feel like a lifetime. When we enter back through the wardrobe, we may have lost some of the maturity we had gained.

But that is the beauty of it all; we were meant to live it out, to find it and lose it, then rediscover it all over again and again and again.

Father is not worried. He has time in His hands and can speed it up if He likes or slow it way down if need be. He is eternal life. When we know Him and Jesus, we have eternal life.

Consider this; our lives are hidden in Christ and we are to seek now those things above where Christ is. So, maybe, this life is the other side of the wardrobe where we are growing up into kings and queens but when we stumble back through into heaven, we are children again, enjoying our loving, heavenly Father.

Scrooge woke up after his night of reclamation and called out eagerly to a young lad on the snow-covered street, "Can you tell me what day this is?"

"What day this is?" replied the lad, "Why it's Christmas of course." Scrooge was overjoyed and marveled; that the ghosts of Christmas had done all their reclamation in one night. Oh joy! He hadn't missed Christmas! How much more can the Holy Spirit do with us? We will not miss our Christmas, either.

Core Scriptures:
1 John 3:2; Revelation 21:5; Hebrews 11:10; Colossians 3:1–4

43

IN AND OUT WE GO

Scrooge's reclamation took place in one night. The children in *The Lion, the Witch and the Wardrobe* lived long lives in Narnia and then, when they stumbled back into their world, it was as though only moments had passed.

We enter, for seasons behind the veil: living in promise, fellowshipping in His word and being transformed from glory to glory. Then something happens—an offense, sin, setback, denial, trauma or drama—and we come tumbling back into the cold reality of life. "Nothing has changed. It is just like I left it," we realize. "I have nothing to show for my life. My hopes and my dreams are gone."

Our vulnerability is greatest when we are in the presence of God, especially during seasons of renewal and revival. We believe, dream, commit to journeys and travel with confidence until something snaps us back to reality and we are left naked with nothing to show for ourselves, hanging on a cross. "He trusted God; let Him save Him," we hear the jeers that Jesus endured but they are not as clear-cut. Our cross seems more circumstantial, the result of our missteps and mistakes. We feel the rejection. We try to forgive and do forgive. We endure our cross as our soul life dies.

"Come down from the cross and we will believe you," the elders taunted Jesus. Why is it that deliverance eludes us? What have we done to deserve such trauma and reproach? The shock of these rude awakenings can be overwhelming. One moment you are in the glorious realm, living, breathing His Holy Spirit, and now you sit in the world with the smell of flesh and its works: confusion and fear. *I've got to do something,* you feel. *This couldn't be God,* you think, and the problem grows because God is silent.

However, God is not silent, just quiet.

His seed is in you—your identity, your nature, and His nature in you. He won't explain everything or keep you from the sufferings that His Son endured. The trouble with the cross it that it is man-made and surrounded by accusation, fear and shame. In stark contrast to the loving, hopeful encouragement of heaven and the presence of God, reasonable requests and subtle mockeries challenge us to perform.

Jesus looked up toward heaven on that cross and in His humanity cried out, "My God, My God, why have you forsaken Me?"

Death is part of the transformation of life. The caterpillar has to cease being a caterpillar in order to become a butterfly. While enjoying the invisible truth of God and even the outward workings of His Spirit, we will endure the cross. It will take our life from us but the seed is sure and the promise complete. Yes and amen to the glory of God through us!

The last words of Jesus on the cross are the most telling: "Into Your hands I commend my spirit." The cross has done its work. It was finished now. Tumbling out of the wardrobe may feel like and be a death of self, vision, dreams and hopes but, where there is death, there is also resurrection. Jesus led many out of prison in His resurrection. So will we:

> When the Lord brought back the captivity of Zion, we were like those who dream. Then our mouth was filled with laughter and our tongue with singing. Then they said among the nations "The Lord has done great things for them." The Lord has done great things for us, and we are glad. (Psalm 126:1–3)

Yes. You stumble and fall but the promises of God are eternal. The divine nature of God calls for resurrection and our habitation is in heaven. In walks Jesus, and there we are again alive, liberated, free in eternity and rejoicing. Our sufferings are a distant memory.

There is less of us but more of Him. The distance between the two worlds has grown shorter.

Core Scriptures:
Matthew 27:42–6; Ephesians 4:7–8; Psalm 126:1–3; John 20:26

44

INTO THE PRESENCE OF GOD

There are many ways into the presence of God—some accidental, others intentional—but every way is in Christ. Jesus said, "I am the way, the truth, and the life. No one comes to the Father except through Me." (John 14:6) He also said, "I am the door. If anyone enters by Me, he will be saved, and will go in and out and find pasture." (John 10:9)

Jesus is the way. He is the door. Through Him, we go in and out and find pasture. Sitting in His presence, I feel His love. I see His grace and enjoy His fellowship. I walk in His promises of the hope behind the veil and am changed into the image of His glory as I behold Him. It is most glorious!

Hebrews 10:19–23 offers us a wonderful image of what we can expect when we intentionally enter into the presence behind the veil. The boldness that allows us to enter in is given to us by the blood of Jesus and our identity in Christ. In this, I remind myself that I am accepted in the Beloved. I come by the righteousness of Christ imputed to me by His blood. I am a child greatly loved, highly favored and I bring much pleasure to my Father. I come there boldly through the door of the new and living way which Jesus consecrated for me in His flesh, death, burial and resurrection, so that where He is, I may be also.

Into the holiest of holies, the inner sanctum of God, I come bounding with joyful acceptance, anticipating my Father's eyes. I run heading straight for my Father's lap. He sits on a throne of grace. Jesus, my high priest, sits with Him or stands before Him there, beckoning me with His eyes. I run toward this enormous, gracious throne that emanates grace and mercy. (The mercy seat that sat on top of the Ark has grown into a throne of grace!)

Oh, the very atmosphere of welcome, provision and help in time of need fills my spiritual senses with hope abounding in the Holy Spirit of God.

Pausing, I step back to look into my glorious Father's face. I say, "My Father, You are glorious. You are kind and loving; giving and forgiving. You abound in goodness and truth. Your mercy is new every morning. You are so gentle and strong. Awesome are your works and your victory is so complete."

I look to Jesus and thank Him again and again for the place He has prepared for me, "Jesus, thank you for being my Savior, Redeemer, Lord and King. You are worthy of all my praise and thanksgiving." This goes on for some time until I feel satisfied that I have blessed my Father and Jesus. This is actually my job description—to minster the fat and the blood. The fat is our praise and the blood our redemption in Christ, and was given as the highest honor before God to the sons of Zadok.

I love my job!

When I feel complete in praise, I approach my Father with my true heart (the state of my soul). Sometimes, whatever had been bothering me is nowhere to be found. Sheepishly I say, "Whatever was bothering me is of no consequence here. Thank you again for my place here."

When I do bring a burden, a soul complaint, I truthfully share my state but do not let that issue separate me from the love of God—because I keep my faith in His blood and in the new and living way He has made for me.

Something wonderful begins to happen. I agree with the blood of Jesus as my heart is sprinkled clean from an evil conscience. What was there is there no longer! I am forgiven; I am free. My conscience is cleansed from dead works (anything that originates outside of Christ or is an addendum to Christ).

Now comes the shower of the water of His word. The Holy Spirit reminds me of scripture. He guides me into truth and the word washes me with pure water. I am sanctified and cleansed.

What a wonderful place!

> Therefore, brethren, having boldness to enter the Holiest by the blood of Jesus, by a new and living way which He consecrated for us, through the veil, that is, His flesh and having a High Priest over the house of God, let us draw near with a true heart in full assurance of faith, having our hearts sprinkled from an evil conscience and our bodies with pure water. Let us hold fast the confession of our hope without wavering for He who promised is faithful. (Hebrews 10:19-23)

Core Scriptures:
John 14:6; 10:9; Hebrews 10:19–23; 9:14; Ezekiel 44:15-16,
Ephesians 5:25–27

45

MY CONFESSION OF HOPE

When I am standing before My Father, sitting in His lap or maybe sitting with Jesus on His throne, in each of these positions, I occupy the same position of sonship, acceptance and rule. Each position is different emotionally and experientially.

Why would we think it strange for the Father to welcome us in His house and speak into our identity in the area of our greatest need? Or His delight? When I am afraid, I find myself in His lap. When I am strong and ready to rule, I may be sitting with Christ. Sometimes, I am simply surprised, finding myself playing and rolling on grassy hills with Jesus.

Our Father and our Lord enjoy our fellowship. God's emotions are wonderful because they are clean, clear, pure, full of love, joy, peace, longsuffering, kindness, goodness, faithfulness, gentleness and self-control. There, His nature saturates my being. I feel these same emotions and soon retain them as mine, partaking of His divine nature.

I then turn to bring Him my confession of hope.

My Father delights in my confession of hope, my confession of salvation in Jesus, and the specific promises that have carried me into this pilgrimage. He is faithful and delights to hear His promises spoken back to Him with rejoicing and confidence, firm until the end. What I have done doesn't matter. Yes, I have bankrupted my promises and wasted my inheritance time and time again. My attempts to bring the promises of God into fruition have only proved my frailty. Yet, He is faithful and does not change.

To enjoy God in my confession of hope is the most amazing discovery I have made in His presence behind the veil. It is eternity, life and inheritance enjoyed, received and taken hold of now. Be prepared, when God starts talking, anyone in faith in His presence—holding fast to their confession of hope—Is liable to hear more! The Holy Spirit has an amazing memory of all that Jesus has said and enjoys sharing it with us.

What is this house Jesus has built for me? Within the very promise He has made now abides a home for me to live in His presence. Although I may tumble out of the wardrobe and find myself back in the stark reality of a cold and cruel world, after a while I smile, knowing I have an abiding city in heaven.

Exploring my confession of hope, my promises and the place Jesus has made for me now are my joyful delight. I am no longer burdened with responsibility to prove or perform—I have only to receive and enjoy. Like a child waiting for Christmas, I live over and over again the coming of that day when faith will become sight. Still, for me, it doesn't matter because faith *has* become my sight. For now, I am saved in this hope and I bring much pleasure to my Father in believing I can abound in hope through the power of the Holy Spirit.

The Holy Spirit is such a helper here. He constantly brings to my remembrance things Jesus has said. "Do you remember when you heard the Lord say this?" He asks.

"Yeah, I do," I say, feeling the same as I had when I first heard that promise and felt the nod of God to go ahead and pick it up. I even remember the circumstances and the expectations I had. Looking at the word He has brought to my remembrance, I might also feel the disappointment of the failure I experienced at the time.

Still, I come with a true heart in full assurance of faith. I am free to talk about my failure but, most of the time, I hear the answer before I ask the question, "It doesn't matter. The promise is true and has you."

The promise itself was the seed of His nature, taking hold of my spirit, imputing His righteousness and nature into mine. "Look at it now," He says, and turning to the word, I see it undefiled, incorruptible and unfading in its glory. In fact, it has grown and become even more glorious. I look and see this great inheritance that the promise has become since the Lord first spoke and beckoned me to believe.

Core Scriptures:
Psalm 16:11; Hebrews 10:23; 3:1–6; Romans 4:17; 8:24–25; 15:13;
1 Peter 1:3–5

46

THE HOUSE JESUS MADE

Jesus built a house by promising us a house! Now, faith is the substance of things hoped for and through His word, He holds the worlds together, framing times and seasons, so that what He says, we become.

On the night of His betrayal, as Jesus prepared to leave His disciples and go to the Father, He said:

> "Let not your heart be troubled; you believe in God, believe also in Me. In My Father's house are many mansions; if it were not so, I would have told you. I go to prepare a place for you. And if I go and prepare a place for you, I will come again and receive you to Myself; that where I am there you may be also." (John 14:1–3)

We are that house! We are the house Jesus went to prepare: "But Christ as a Son over His own house, whose house we are, if we hold fast the confidence and the rejoicing of the hope firm to the end." (Hebrews 3:6). Imagine we are the house of God being built up into a holy habitation for God in the Spirit. There is going to be a wedding and we are the bride, the holy city, the New Jerusalem.

That night, Judas questioned Jesus, "How in the world can You reveal yourself to us and not the rest of the world?" Jesus answered, 'If anyone loves Me, he will keep My word; and My Father will love him and We will come to him and make Our home with him.'" (John 14:23).

In order to draw the rich habitation promised to us, there are two important things to understand from this passage. First is "Keep My word" means to *watch* it, not *do* it. We get so messed up with this proud outlook toward scripture. We are commanded to "watch," that is, to observe and look after, to keep it before us, prize and believe it.

Jesus' words are living. Jesus did only what He saw His Father doing. So we are to look intently into the mirror and then we, too, can do what we see our Father doing.

While we give place to watching over His word, our Father loves and desires to dwell in the midst of our watching over His word. We become His home. This is the second important aspect of this passage. "Home" is the same Greek word translated as "mansions" as we read earlier in John 14:2.

So, to help our thinking, let's switch the English words and paraphrase these two verses: "In My Father's house are many mansions... and We will come to Him and make our mansion with Him." We are the Father's many mansions! We are His dwelling place in the Spirit on earth as He is our dwelling place in the Spirit in heaven.

Having been freed from performing and called to sit with Christ, I began to realize that the promises God made to me so long ago were indeed His place of residence within me. At first, I couldn't explain this, I was still in the doing mind-set and all of my failure to achieve had left me a bit traumatized.

Yet, as I became acclimated to sitting in His presence and not striving outside of it, I could see that I was called to sit with Christ. Through entering into the presence behind the veil through Christ, I was called not only to enjoy Christ but to live there with Him.

His word is living, abiding and a place where God dwells. His promises are my dwelling place, my partaking of His divine nature. "If you abide in Me and My words abide in you..."

When the Father promises me something, it is to create a place in which to dwell through faith while partaking of His divine nature. The outcome that we want and need are not the primary reason the Father had spoken. Rather, He speaks to make space in us for Him. The Father promised us a house.

I went to find that house, failed in my attempt to gain it but then discovered that I *was* the house.

Core Scriptures:
John 14:1–3; Hebrews 3:6; 11:10; John 14:23; James 1:23–5; John 15:7

47

SEEING IS DOING

Jesus only did what He saw His Father do. Whenever a man turns to Christ, the veil is removed from His heart. Now we can see, and with unveiled faces, we behold in a mirror the glory of the Lord and are transformed into that same image from glory to glory.

That is why we just can't do the word. First, we are to turn to it. Glory is not something we do. It is something we become. The entrance of His word gives light and, in His light, we see light.

Still, it takes some time to develop into the full image we see. Hearing revelation and then immediately acting on it is the same as Peter trying to counsel Jesus not to die on the cross, after receiving the revelation that Jesus was the Son of the living God. We just do not get it all the first time through.

Fear makes us act, and I was a doer. I could see the Lord in so much of what was being said, preached, prophesied and sung but rather than worship and *become*, I would do and fall flat on my face, wondering what had happened.

It doesn't help either when others are telling you, "Do...do...do." The urgency of obedience seems so noble but it leaves you so empty.

The word is living and a discerner of thoughts and intentions of the heart. The word carries the life of God and we should value it before we act upon it. My years of action had left me disillusioned but, like Peter, I was stuck. I had come to know that Jesus had the words of eternal life and that He was the Christ, but where was I to go next?

So many times my Papa would nod and say, "Go ahead. Pick that up, Steve. That's a really good promise for you and it is what I am doing right now." You bet I picked it up and, with sincerity and conviction, I went to do what the promise said it would do.

But God didn't say, "Do it." He said, "Pick it up."

The handling of the word in the presence of the Lord is the confession of hope that transforms us through the beholding of His glory. I would hear and obey without having the capacity to obey—only mimic. But the word had been sown and my life captured. This word in the womb of my spirit waited to grow and become me. That's right, *become me*; the word becomes flesh as it did before, consuming us in the glory of the Lord.

Now I sit and enter into the promises that I have been given through the Holy Spirit (Who has the authority to remind, guide, reveal and enlarge all that Jesus has said). The Father has given all things to Jesus and Jesus has given all things to us. The Holy Spirit is our guide, revealer, helper, reminder and everything we need to see.

In the midst of His promises are living oracles and eternal substance. There, in His word, I dwell. I walk the width and breadth of the promises as I sing and run through the word, laughing at the enormity of what God has said. His word is light and the universe is expanding at the speed of light. Imagine what the source of light is doing within our hearts – if we will stop and see.

When Isaiah saw the glory of the Lord, he was undone but after the coal touched his lips, he was commissioned to go and preach, his message being,

> Go and tell this people: 'keep on hearing, but do not understand; keep on seeing, but do not perceive. Make the heart of this people dull, and their ears heavy, and shut their eyes; lest they see with their eyes, and hear with their ears and understand with their heart, and return and be healed.'" (Isaiah 6:9–10)

Isaiah saw, and his life and ministry were changed forever. In fact, all he could see from that point on was Jesus; he kept prophesying Jesus, so much so that Jesus quoted him in every gospel and explained the reason for His parables by this verse in Isaiah.

Don't be in a hurry to do. Take the time to see.

Core Scriptures:
John 5:19–20; II Corinthians 3:16; Matthew 13:10–17; 16:16-23;
John 6:68-69; Hebrews 4:12; Isaiah 6:1–10

48

FIVE LOAVES AND TWO FISH

In 1999, in the midst of our church's revival, I had an experience in a prayer meeting that felt like I was giving the Lord my five loaves and two fishes (my lunch). Or maybe it was similar to the way Mary felt when she poured her alabaster oil on Jesus' head.

Here is what I wrote in my journal the night of October 4, 1999.

> We have all labored long and hard, but have only a piece. Give it all to Jesus, and let Him bless it and feed the multitudes. We came to the altar to give to Jesus all that we have, have completed, possess, and have right to—all our prayers and authorities. For Jesus to look to heaven to bless, break, and give to the disciples is to give to the multitudes.

> This giving continues to include everything we possess, every promise ever made, and every gift ever given (we pour these out to the Lord). Then we step back from, "I give to You," to behold, "I am."

> The glory of God fell into the room and everyone began to sing and worship. Some fell to the ground, others bowed, and others moved about in worship and with flags.

The glory became stronger and stronger until we could sing no more and only be silent, for anything said might be irreverent; except when glory built up and we needed to praise or else explode, for, "His is the kingdom and the power and the glory forever."

This vivid moment stands still for me, because it was the handing over of my little lunch of five loaves and two fishes. I wish I could have seen an immediate miracle of multiplication but I began to see death instead. Three days later, a dear sister in our church passed away after a long battle with cancer. By the weekend, I was doing a funeral in glory.

What happens when God initiates these kinds of transactions on the earth in heaven? When people give their lives to the Lord in a profound moment of exchange, the word of the Lord activates faith to come and follow Him and leaving all, they arise and go.

We sell the farm and off we go but, instead of victory, death comes. Did we miss it? Did we fail to have faith? Didn't we pray hard enough or act wisely enough? Maybe, probably, who knows? It all turns to vapor or does it?

In heaven, all glorious transactions of faith—rising to follow, leaving all, selling the farm without a backup plan—are sacred and revered. They are holy to God because they are faith. These transactions please Him, even if we stumble and fall, or the devil breaks in and steals, or if we are not prudent.

Six days before the Passover, Mary took a pound of very costly oil of spikenard and anointed Jesus' feet. He received the act of faith and love. While others did not understand and ridiculed such display of emotion, not the Lord. He received Mary's abandoned worship as a prophetic act for His burial and declared it to be a memorial in heaven, recorded in the gospel to be returned to and rewarded.

In the years that followed that October evening, I had two feelings about it. First, I was extremely grateful that I had given the Lord my little lunch before it all exploded and went away. I felt that I had deposited something precious and valuable into the Lord's hand.

Second, I wondered, *Whatever happened to Mary after that special night?* After giving away her dowry, the pound of costly oil (worth a year's wages), did she suffer financially? Did she ever doubt the wisdom of such extravagant worship? Sitting alone with her thoughts, she might have wondered, *What have I done?*

I know I did. Eleven years later, I would find out what I had done.

Core Scriptures:
Mark 6:30–44; Matthew 26:6–13; John 12:1–8

49

MY LUNCH HAD BECOME A MANSION

In June of 2010, I was sitting in the sanctuary of our church. I was in the Spirit when the heavens opened up and I saw a vision of heaven and my Father's house. For two hours, I walked about inside this vision and saw the treasuries of God—His storehouses of gold, silver, hail, lighting, snow and grace.

Below are some excerpts from my journal that day.

> I saw that in my Father's house are many mansions, many rooms. I saw mine titled "abundant life." I entered, and I saw God had provided me with everything I needed for life and godliness. I saw rooms filled with gold, others with silver, diamonds, hail, snow, and lighting.

> I saw such an abundance of grace. The grace was just continuing to grow; it never depleted, only increased. Every morning, like manna—"fresh-baked grace"—I saw healings, jobs, covenants renewed, messages and whatever was needed, more than enough for the whole congregation.

> As I moved around my house and felt this abundance of God's riches, I praised God and shouted, "This is my lunch!" My little bag of two fishes and five loaves, the little revival I gave to Jesus

in October 1999 had grown and multiplied a thousand times, and now it was a mansion filled with the riches of Christ. It was my mansion.

I fell out of my chair and in utter ecstasy shouted, travailed, "This is it! This is my reward, my mansion, my authority, my destiny. I will release a nation; nations will be fed the abundance of Christ—both in plenty and in famine. I will be like Joshua and bring His people into the inheritance He has sworn to them."

Yes. In my Father's house are the promises, the covenants He has made. They sit in His presence. When we enter into the presence behind the veil, the Holy Spirit communicates to us our promises, His covenants, and we fellowship at the throne of grace.

Everything is here at the throne of grace; everything God has ever spoken is there in the presence behind the veil. Nothing is lost; only sin has been forgotten; only our sins are not there. They have been thrown into the sea of forgetfulness.

They are forgotten, but not our suffering. Our suffering is most precious, it is the offering God holds as precious. He holds every tear, every broken heart and crushed life with the sufferings of His Son. They are together; they have increased in wealth and therefore the inheritance is that much greater. The sorrows, sufferings, pains are all there. He even places the tears He wipes away inside a bottle.

This struggle of faith is our true offering. It is where we give to Him our love and faith. I see the Father sitting on His throne and at His right hand are the covenants/promises He has made; at His left hand is the suffering we have endured. Faith and love. His precious promises, our precious faith. His love and suffering for us. Our love for Him and our suffering with Him.

The Father holds His promises as covenants made to us; our sufferings as love towards Him. Suffering is not a requirement to inheritance—just a hazard of the job. Father looks into time before He speaks into our lives, seeing the effect His word will have on us as we struggle to live out His promise. He sees the warfare that will come to displace His seed in us but in His confidence says, "I can do that. I can bring the promise to pass and I will."

He never promises what He is not able to perform in us. No matter what happens to us, the promise is sure as well as the end that is intended by the Lord.

Who knows what your lunch has become in the Father's house? I know one thing. It is not lost.

Core Scriptures:
Revelation 1:10; Job 38:22; Hebrews 6:17–20; Psalm 56:8; 69:29–33;
Romans 4:41

50

LIVING LARGE IN GOD

J oy, freedom and complete abandonment are in His presence. Christ's finished work has an air of confidence not found on earth. There are no problems in heaven, only grace, grace and more grace. The Lord has won. The Lamb has overcome!

When you spend time in heaven, your perspective and attitude change. The urgency that so often accompanies our labor here on earth does not exist in heaven. Rest rules. The sea is glassy and calm; all eyes are on Jesus.

After I found myself living from within the heavenly realm, I soon lost my earthly sense of urgency. I laughed at myself and my former ideas. Imagine heaven grinding to a halt and everyone looking around. "What's the matter?" someone asks. "Humanity has failed," the angel replies. Heaven has come to a standstill. "We can do nothing now until humanity gets its act together."

He who sits in heaven laughs at the antics of humankind. Nothing we do can threaten God's peace or interrupt His rest. Jesus slept on the pillow in the back of the boat during a windstorm that so freaked out His disciples (many of whom were experienced sailors) that they woke up the Lord and accused Him of not caring about their sure death.

That is us down here. That's me. I know the Bible says we are "fearfully and wonderfully made," but most of the time, I am just "fearful." I look around to see the nations raging, people plotting, taking counsel together against the Lord and His anointed and I fear. Yet, "He who sits in heaven shall laugh; The Lord shall hold them in derision" (Psalm 2:4).

But what does He do after He stops laughing?

He just goes ahead establishing His rule in greater brilliance and clarity, setting His King on His holy hill in Zion. He decrees, "You are My Son, today I have begotten You." Right as the nations rage, right in the middle of our mess, right in the middle of the storm, right in the middle of my fear, He decrees, "You are My Son; today I have begotten You."

Yes. "You are a son of the most high God," the Holy Spirit answers the decree. This is sonship in the midst of warfare but it gets better. God decrees our inheritance, "Ask of Me and I will give You the nations for Your inheritance and the ends of the earth for Your possession." The Father says to me, "Ask and I will give inheritance and possession. I am in a giving mood." What a different place heaven is from earth. It is nearly its exact opposite.

You can see why spending time in His presence will allow you to see the world differently. You may just start sleeping more during storms, laughing more during uprisings and experiencing major identity-affirming moments. You might find yourself dancing in the midst of disciples who tell you of great exploits in God.

Rejoicing and twirling around you say, "I thank you, Father, for revealing your kingdom to us babes. For giving us what the wise and prudent couldn't see. For giving us the kingdom." With childlike faith you sing, "I love my Father. I love my Jesus. I love what the Lord is doing now!"

You're outside of the box! You are living large in the kingdom.

Oops, someone is watching you. "What are you so happy about?" they ask.

Your response? "I am redeemed. I am saved. I am alive. I am loved and have been given an inheritance in God. I am His inheritance."

Core Scriptures:
Revelation 4–6; 15:2; Mark 4:36–9; Revelation 5:6–14;
Psalm 2:4–9; 139:14; Luke 10:21–4

51

SIT HERE

Did you know that sitting is ruling? That's right. Since Jesus' resurrection, He has been sitting and waiting until the Father makes His enemies His footstool. I know everyone tells us that it is *our* job to make all of Jesus' enemies His footstool. Still, the Bible just doesn't say that and I am glad because, if it is up to me, Jesus is going to be sitting for a *long* time.

"You prepared a table for me in the presence of my enemies," David said. Do you realize how hard it is to sit and eat in the presence of your enemies? But that is the way to enforce God's rule—by sitting in the midst of upheaval, instead of running around crying, "The sky is falling."

In his maturity, David later saw much behind the veil as he fellowshipped with the Lord and heard God's promise of Jesus. In Psalm 110:1–2, David wrote:

> The Lord said to my Lord, "Sit at My right hand, till I make Your enemies Your footstool." The Lord shall send the rod of Your strength out of Zion. Rule in the midst of Your enemies!

Sitting and ruling go hand in hand.

When the Lord called me to sit with Him, I laughed with Him at what had previously threatened, irritated or frightened me. I enjoyed the joke that was on me. Now, I laugh more at myself these days than at anything else.

When you stop taking yourself so seriously, move out of fear and control, and rest in His love, you learn to laugh at yourself. After sitting with Christ on His throne—with His promises my dwelling place, His blood my identity, His love my portion—my perspective changed.

"What do you want me to do besides laugh?" I asked early on during my five-month internship in heaven.

"I want you to sit here until I make your enemies your footstool, in My Son Jesus," the Father replied sternly but gently with a hint of joy.

"Sit, do nothing?" It made no sense. If it had not been for my many failed attempts to bring God's promises to pass (and if I had not so completely moved from my earthly to this heavenly dwelling), I think I would have argued the wisdom of such a strategy. As I meditated and received these instructions, I began to see the wisdom of God.

When I sit, I sit in Christ and declare in that action that Christ has completed the work that is currently in contest. Whenever I leave my seat of authority, given to me by my Father, I move into striving, fear and failure. I have to resort to control and law to secure what has already been given me.

There is no contest. Jesus is Lord. Every knee shall bow and every tongue will confess that Jesus Christ is Lord to the glory of God the

Father. One day, this will be done. Then Jesus will return the authority back to the Father.

> Now, then all things are made subject to Him, when the Son Himself will also be subject to Him who put all things under Him, that God may be all in all. (I Corinthians 15:28)

When we sit with Him, we rule with Him. When we become terrified, frightened and controlling, we stumble out of our reign. When we are sitting, we are ruling. That's why Paul exhorted the Philippians, "...and not in any way terrified by your adversaries, which is to them a proof of perdition, but to you of salvation and that from God." (Philippians 1:28).

I spend a lot of time laughing, which keeps me sitting in heaven. I sit in the expectation of the completion of all promises in Christ. I dwell in His promises, partaking of His divine nature, becoming His dwelling place. His mansion and His promises also become my dwelling place—my mansion.

I praise. I play. I dance and reign in the midst of my enemies as a priest on earth seated with Christ in heavenly places.

Core Scriptures:
Hebrews 1:3, 13; Psalm 23:5; Psalm 110:1–2; 23:5; 1 Corinthians 15:24–8;
Philippians 1:28

52

WALKING IN THE COOL OF THE DAY

Walking in the cool of the day, the Lord would visit Adam. This is better translated as "in the wind of the Spirit, the Lord would walk with Adam."

In heaven, all things agree with God and walk together in oneness. When I sit with Christ on His throne, especially after any "enduring of the cross," I find that the voice of God is so wonderful to bring me into fellowship with the completed work of the cross. "It is finished," the Lord will say, "and so it is finished." There is nothing to be added—only enjoyed.

Still, anxiety is subtle fear and grips my heart too often.

Sitting in the ocean on my surfboard, I struggled with a sense of separation from His love. So I sought the Lord, asking "What was this?" That was when the Lord said to me, "All separation is an awareness of nakedness that brings fear of punishment. Who or what told you that you were naked?"

As I thought about this, I saw the truth of it. Fear has torment and fear fuels lust, just as love is security and produces faith. Why was I afraid? Who told me I was naked? What did I fear?

Often, separation and fear are subtle and it is difficult to discern the source of such feelings. They can accompany long periods of stress, work or constant attention to anything (as our gaze shifts from His acceptance and love in Christ to our own effort and work).

"Baptize me in Your love," I prayed and soon found love, His liquid love, flowing into my empty heart. The Holy Spirit pours God's love into our hearts and there is a never-ending supply of such love. All we need to do is ask. "Come sit with Me," I heard the Father say. "What is it that you have that I cannot help you with? What are you trying to do that I am not able to do?" Questions are locators and the Father, through the Holy Spirit, is so good at asking questions.

"I don't know what it is. Or it is this fear of not having enough of...?" I answered.

"Well, then let it go," the Father would say. "Cast this care to Me, because I care for you."

Oh, the wonders of His voice and the freedom it brings. Scripture comes to life with the voice of God answering an honest heart. It changes everything inside. Our struggle is often internal. We struggle to rest and submit to His promises in the face of our problems. We shift our hearts from faith to lust, out of love to fear.

It happens every time my heart shifts from faith or love as I become more aware of my circumstances on earth and not my seat in Christ. By the time I realize what is happening, I have tried all the usual remedies, more prayer and more work.

But the problem was perception. I believed a lie—the lie that I am *not* loved, cared for, watched and fussed over or delighted in. I have shifted from son to servant—from heir to hireling. I was working to gain what had already been given.

Sitting in heaven has become a place of dwelling in Christ for me. I have always prayed a lot but, in the past, so often I would pray to be allowed to bring whatever I saw of God back to the earth. Now? I sit and enjoy the work accomplished in Christ, taking time to enter into it in heaven in the Spirit.

This is the oneness that Jesus enjoyed with the Father, the oneness now promised us—that we would be one in His love and one in His glory, the word sanctifying us, His love settling us and His glory transforming us.

When we are struggling to maintain our fellowship—the temptations to break it, whether subtle or very overt—God's promises hold us in His Spirit and impart to us eternal life, knowing God. Yes, I laugh a lot these days and enjoy the Lord in His completeness. I don't want to move from this place of rest here in His love.

Core Scriptures:
Genesis 3:8; Hebrews 12:1–2; 1 John 4:17–29; Romans 5:5;
1 Peter 5:7; John 17:21–23

53

ONENESS CANNOT BE DIVIDED

Oneness is the unity that God is. He is never divided, anxious, intimidated, frightened or challenged. He is God. He is one and He is whole. The Lord is one God—Father, Son, and Holy Spirit. We are made in His image—spirit, soul, and body—and we are being sanctified wholly. We are wholly His, now and forever.

So everything of yours is His and everything of His is yours. We are one in Christ and He is one in us—not by works of righteousness that we have done but by His work alone. In Christ, we live, move and exist.

When the Lord called me to heaven to sit with Him intentionally and forever, I had long ago exhausted the belief that I could make God do anything or that I needed to do something in order to prompt the Lord's action. I had visited the Lord so many times in prayer, worship and in His word. I enjoyed His presence and He would give me His promises over and over again, making my life full of faith and frustration.

I could see the word and hear the word but could not *do* the word. What was wrong with me? Why couldn't I bring the Lord's promises to pass? Why could I not bring change where the Lord promised change?

I think I have practiced every manner of faithful exercise and prophetic action possible. But my heart would condemn me when I moved further from the finished work and into something I felt I needed to do for the Lord so that He could do what He had promised. Promises come through the voice of His Spirit. The Spirit brings faith and hope and we move forward in obedience. But our actions are not sufficient to accomplish the promise, and we can soon find ourselves struggling to make things happen. The Holy Spirit promises that God will inhabit us by faith if we make room for Him. The performance of the promise is His to accomplish.

When Abraham came into the final year of his twenty-five year journey of waiting for the promise of Isaac to be realized, he no longer strove to accomplish what the Lord had promised. Abraham moved with faith and also moved in fear when he saw King Abimelech.

Abraham feared that the king would kill him and take his wife Sarah for his own wife. So he lied about their relationship. Sure enough, someone pointed out the beautiful Sarah. The next thing Abraham knew, Sarah was in King Abimelech's house waiting to become his wife.

In my mind, that would be grounds enough for the promise to be withdrawn or at least postponed while Abraham went through some inner healing or deliverance from fear but God thought differently. God simply woke up King Abimelech one night and told him that he was a dead man.

"Why?" the startled king asked.

"Because the woman you have is the wife of Abraham," was the Lord's reply.

"He never told me nor did she," the fearful king uttered in desperation.

"I know. That is why I woke you up, to tell you," the Lord said. "But if you don't restore Abraham's wife, you and your household are dead. Furthermore, Abraham will pray for you, for he is a prophet, to heal the barrenness that has entered into your household as a result of your actions," the Lord promised.

Sarah was restored. Abraham explained his fear to King Abimelech, prayed for his household and they were healed. Abraham was given free reign of the land.

Why? Because the Lord had a set time to accomplish His promise to Abraham. The divine nature of faith in regard to Isaac was completed. Abraham was fully convinced of the Lord's ability to perform His promise, even in the face of his own fear.

Core Scriptures:
1 Thessalonians 5:23; Galatians 3:1–14; Romans 4:21; Genesis 20

54

FAITH IS NOT CONTROL

Abraham did not control circumstances to make sure that, by the next spring, God would fulfill his promise of Isaac. That was settled. However, his fear for his own safety was still an issue.

Abraham was not rewarded because of his morality or outstanding character but because of his faith. He believed God was able to perform what He had promised. He spent the time—even, years—learning God's voice and, in His presence, he believed, heard the wonderful promise of inheritance and dwelt there in it. Behind the veil, Abraham dwelt in His presence.

When the day came on the Lord's calendar to call the promise into fulfillment, Abraham didn't take himself seriously as a factor in its completion. It was God who promised and God would perform the promise. Abraham looked at his dead body (he was almost one hundred years old) and Sarah's dead womb (that had never carried life before) and said, "The Lord has spoken; I agree. I will praise Him and glorify Him."

Abraham didn't even make it a priority to convince Sarah. The Lord Himself made a trip to Abraham's house to speak in Sarah's hearing that Isaac would be born in a year. Jesus (who I believe was the angel of the Lord) and two other angels restated the promise to Abraham as Sarah listened from the doorway of her tent.

Sarah laughed within herself saying, "After I have grown old, shall I have pleasure, my lord being old also?"(Genesis 18:12) The Lord heard this and asked Abraham why Sarah had laughed. Was anything too hard for the Lord? Abraham stayed out of it. Sarah denied that she had laughed but the Lord said she had and left it at that.

Abraham, Sarah and their entire household moved after the destruction of Sodom and Gomorrah and dwelt in Abimelech's kingdom. They lied about their relationship, were delivered from their sin and, within a year, Isaac was born. This is the father of our faith.

Abraham and Sarah's faith pleased God; and it is the goodness of God that He will do what He says, in spite of what we do. I know, I have erroneously believed that I had to do such-and-such in order for the Lord to do what He had promised; or I believed that because I had done such-and-such the Lord could not fulfill His promise.

Both ways of thinking are not acts of faith. They are prideful, fearful attempts to explain patience as a qualifier for the Lord's movement. Patience is not an achievement but an act of surrender and, when it has its perfect work, we are complete, lacking nothing.

Patience is changing us, yes, but not into outstanding moral citizens who deserve God's mercy, but rather, into trusting sons and daughters who rest complete in the finished work of Christ, knowing that our actions determine nothing.

His promises are His to perform. Our role is to receive and trust that even in the unsanctified areas of our lives, God will protect us. God does not want us to return to the Law of Moses as the basis of our relationship and live in fear and torment as servants instead of children. Sitting with Christ is the closest place we can come to experiencing the rest of faith every day. We practice His presence, and hold our confession of hope steadfast, because He who promised is faithful to perform.

We just don't know when nor should we care. Sitting in His presence behind the veil is our inheritance now. We are not meant to accomplish anything but to rest in everything.

The dramatic way in which the Lord called me into His presence, to sit with Him on His throne and laugh, was my Isaac moment. It was long preceded by learning and knowing His voice. My greatest challenge has been to not add anything nor let my humanity become my focal point and disqualify me from being here.

Core Scriptures:
Romans 4:17–22; Genesis 18:1–15; James 1:2–4; Hebrews 10:23

55

ENJOYING GOD NOW

Enjoying God is not frivolousness or irresponsibility; It is faith and a delight to our Father.

The promises that bring us into faith and fellowship, along with the struggle and division in our own souls, have already been accomplished in Christ. There is no question about the Lord's fulfillment.

It may take place after we die. It may be seen in heaven or on earth generations away. Still, it is already done. The promise is our access to fellowship in His presence behind the veil. It's our meeting point, His dwelling place in us.

When I experienced this call up to heaven to sit with Christ, I enjoyed the Lord in His fullness and His finished work, laughing, playing and dancing all the time. It felt like heaven. After five months, when the Lord gave me permission to teach and explain the presence behind the veil, I could sense the appearance of striving within myself.

How could I bring people in? What should I explain? How should I do this? Well, I couldn't. I could only share what I had seen and let the Lord determine the outcome. I could not make God do something He was not ready to do. I had failed enough in attempting to perform His promises and I had learned to rest without others sharing my vision.

His glory affects the beholders and transforms them, making them messengers of His glory. Unless the Lord reveals Himself in the message, your words are heard but not heard, seen but not seen. We are like Isaiah, who was commissioned after his heavenly experience to go and tell the people that in seeing, they would not see; in hearing, they would not hear; nor would they understand with their hearts unless they should see with their eyes, hear with their ears, understand with their hearts and turn to the Lord so that He could heal them.

How would it feel to experience the glory of the Lord and have to tell others that they would not be able to receive it? Well, it didn't bother Isaiah, because from that point on, he just told what he heard and kept gazing into heaven to see what heaven was doing.

Isaiah saw Jesus. He saw His death, burial and resurrection. Isaiah saw the New Jerusalem and the redemption of Israel. He saw God saving, healing and restoring. Isaiah saw the highway of holiness and the ransomed of the Lord returning, singing and laughing with everlasting joy. He saw the Creator God, Savior God, Redeemer God and the Mighty One of Israel.

With all this, Isaiah didn't let the reception of his message keep him from hearing, seeing and telling more. Isaiah, like Abraham, had entered into the promises of God.

Life is inside the presence behind the veil—where Christ our forerunner has entered and where we are invited to live—Not visit, but live. Our citizenship is in heaven. I have a place prepared for me in heaven now in Christ. God has a place prepared for Himself now in me.

Living from this place in the Spirit is incredible. I feel righteousness, peace and joy in the Holy Spirit. The victory has been won. Death has been conquered and nothing can separate us from God's love. It is a glorious thing that we have been joined into oneness in God, not by works of righteousness which we have done but by grace through faith in Christ, a salvation so rich and so free. We are seated with Christ—His trophies of grace, His workmanship. And in the ages to come, He will show the riches of His grace in His kindness toward us.

How far can we explore? How much can we know? I don't think anyone knows. I am sure no one has reached the depths of His love or the riches of His grace and glory. Maybe you could be the first, like Enoch, and walk with God until you are not.

And Enoch walked with God; and he was not, for God took him. (Genesis 5:24)

Core Scriptures:
Hebrews 6:13–20; Isaiah 6:8–13; 53; 35; 43:1–7; Philippians 3:20; Romans 14:17; Ephesians 2:6–10; Genesis 5:24

56

WALKING WITH GOD

I was saved out of fear. I was living in fear. Fear is an awful thing because it involves torment—a threat of punishment and rejection. It is a tormentor that causes us to live in regret and shame. Just as Adam covered his nakedness, our fear causes us to hide from the One who can save us.

There are no regrets or fears in heaven because heaven has fully redeemed all things. The blood of Christ has made all things new: all things are perfect and complete. Even our most shameful acts are now trophies to His grace. The horrific things done to us are doors that have opened an experience into His grace, unparalleled to anything here.

In heaven, there simply are no regrets because everything has led to Jesus, and Jesus has redeemed everything to Himself. He has become all things and fills all things. The thing we hated has become our door into Christ. It drove us to find Him.

Walking with God is the same. It is a pilgrimage that is unparalleled to anything we can experience on earth. In fact, it is out of this world. We are invited to walk with God in His heavenly places so that we can demonstrate God in our earthly places.

This is not a play on words. Who's your daddy? Where is your home? If your daddy is from earth and your home is here, you will find Christ as a source of hope for change. If your Daddy is in heaven and your home is in heaven, you will walk on earth with an air of confidence in the invisible, knowing that the active will of God is in all things and is good. You will become less and less subject to the beggarly principles of this life. You will not rebel against them but submit to them. In submission, you will yield and become completely free.

Walking with God moves you out of this world into pilgrimage. Your promises become your promised land of which your Father is the architect and builder. In heaven, there is no struggle with earth. Heaven is not in a wrestling match trying to get the upper hand. Rather, it is in joyful celebration of Christ and His overcoming bride.

Heaven is preparing for a marriage, adorning the Lamb with praise and awaiting the maturity of the bride—while being confident in the finished work of Christ. That is why joy and laughter are so easy in heaven. There are no regrets, only salvation. There is no striving, only rest. There is no agitation, only peace, the peace of God.

It has been over a year since the Lord called me up to sit with Him on His throne as He sits with His Father. This sovereign act of God, preceded by so many visits and invitations, failures, fears, losses and revelations, has swallowed up all my past sufferings, confusion, sorrow and loss.

Now, I look at Him who is invisible, instead of the temporal world. That's right. No matter how sovereign an act, it is meant to be occupied by us. Jesus has prepared a place for us and the Greek word, "place" implies "a place that is occupied," something that is yours because you are using it.

"Excuse me, but that is my chair," I might say to someone at a dinner party. "Why?" they ask, and I answer, "It is my chair because I was using it."

The idea of walking with God is creating a path, a worn path, through much travel. That is what Enoch did. He walked with God until he was not. God took Enoch because he had pleased God by faith. I can see the Lord saying to Enoch, "Enoch, you spend so much time here walking amongst the things of God, the fiery stones and those who dwell here. Why don't you stay here and be no more in the world?"

Enoch had lived in the presence behind the veil. He had walked with God and now he was "not on earth."

Core Scriptures:
1 John 4:17–19; Genesis 3:10; Hebrews 11:8–16; John 14:2–3;
Genesis 5:24

57

IN THIS WORLD BUT NOT OF IT

We are called to live in this world but not to live from it. Our life is in Christ and hidden there.

I have been crucified with Christ; it is no longer I who live, but Christ lives in me; and the life which I now live in the flesh I live by faith in the Son of God, who loved me and gave Himself for me. (Galatians 2:20)

OK. So how do we do that?

By beholding Christ, we are to seek those things above where Christ is seated at the right hand of God. We are to behold, as in a mirror, the glory of the Lord in the face of Jesus Christ, and be transformed into that image from glory to glory.

Knowing our point of origin determines our identity. It is all about the questions, "Who is our daddy?" and "Where is our home?" Our Father is in heaven and our home is there also. Why should it be strange then, that we are told in the word to seek the kingdom of heaven and its righteousness, and all other things will be added to us?

I used to think that verse meant, "Seek God's kingdom first and then my stuff here on earth would be taken care of because I had put the kingdom first." Now I know it to mean, "Seek God's kingdom in heaven and its rule will be enforced in my life on earth." My home is heaven; my destiny is the glory of God. I know that the New Jerusalem will be here on the new earth but it first comes down from heaven.

Jesus said His kingdom was not of this world or His servants would have fought to rescue Him from the rule of Pontius Pilate and the Jews' desire to crucify Him.

Let's listen to what He said to Pontius Pilate:

> Jesus answered, "My kingdom is not of this world. If My kingdom were of this world, My servants would fight, so that I should not be delivered to the Jews; but now My Kingdom is not from here." Pilate therefore said to Him, "Are You a king then?" Jesus answered, "You say rightly that I am a king. For this cause I was born, and for this cause I have come into the world, that I should bear witness to the truth. Everyone who is of the truth hears My voice." (John 18:36–37)

My problem has always been trying to make this world my home in Christ. When the cross comes (that intersection of God's greater intention versus my intention), I fight not to be delivered and don't ask what the Lord is doing in the moment. Instead, I deliver myself, if possible.

Trust is the essence of faith. Hope and love combine in one beautiful rest in God. The Lord did not fight the circumstances or defend

Himself in that Hall of Justice. He just kept committing Himself to the One who judges righteously. My greatest failures in faith occurred when I sought to save my life.

Joseph became free when he let go of his confession of himself: "I am a Hebrew having been stolen from my land and wrongly imprisoned in this dungeon." So when the time came that he was presented before Pharaoh, he could enter into those radical shifts without his old identity or old grievances getting in the way. He shaved his beard and dressed as an Egyptian. He was given an Egyptian name and an Egyptian wife, the daughter of Poti-Pherah. In fact, Joseph looked so Egyptian that his brothers didn't recognize him when they arrived.

Paul was not delivered from prison until he started using his Roman citizenship to deliver himself from unjust punishment. It brought temporary relief but also dragged him deeper and deeper into the Roman system. God used prison in Paul's life to increase his writing career, which has benefited all of us.

The point is simply that using our rights, which link us to this world, does not always give witness to the truths we carry. We have to know the kingdom we are in and how to walk in the liberty of Christ.

Core Scriptures:
Galatians 2:20; Colossians 3:1–4; 2 Corinthians 3:18; Matthew 7:33;
Revelation 21:2; John 18:36–7; 1 Peter 2:21–3; Genesis 40:14–15

58

KNOWING CHRIST BY THE SPIRIT

When we enter into the presence behind the veil, we enter into the Spirit and not the flesh. We leave the limitations of our natural man, our carnal nature, and are made alive in the Spirit. Living before the Lord in the fellowship of His Spirit, we become one in His nature. Through His promises, we partake of His divine nature. Having escaped the corruption of the flesh, we walk by faith, not by sight.

It is great. There is so much you can enjoy with God if you don't have to prove anything.

Jesus said that many kings and prophets had desired to see what the disciples were seeing. Yet, the disciples didn't even know what they were seeing. The angels longed to look into salvation but could not. Prophets of old inquired and searched carefully, in the Spirit, to try to determine Christ's sufferings and ultimate glories that would follow.

Everyone who is spiritual wants to see into the salvation that has been given to us but these things are not revealed by flesh and blood, nor can flesh and blood inherit the kingdom. Sooner or later, we must let go of trying to bring Christ into the flesh. Instead, we must live with Christ in the Spirit.

Jesus told His disciples that the Father was always with Him. Yet they could not see the Father or know what He was talking about. The Holy Spirit opens our eyes to see, hear and understand what the Lord has prepared for us. We are to know one another by the Spirit, not the flesh.

It doesn't matter how smart or wonderful someone is in church. If that person has not yielded his or her life to the Spirit of God, he or she is being ruled by flesh. Such people live in strife, division and envy. Said another way, "childish." Now, to be *childish* is to behave like mere men. To be *childlike* means to have a simple, sincere faith that beholds Jesus as a child does (without guile, doubt or mixed motives).

Of course, we all have guile, doubts and mixed motives but, as we walk in the Spirit, we become less and less flesh-impressed and more and more Spirit-impressed. The Holy Spirit becomes our guide, comforter, helper and interpreter of everything, helping us to understand the voice of God and live in peace and joy.

Now, the fruit of the Spirit is the divine attribute of God's blessing and abundance, reproducing in our daily life. Love, joy, peace, longsuffering, kindness, goodness, faithfulness, gentleness and self-control are these fruits of the Spirit which are seen and enjoyed in us before they are seen by others.

When I understood this through the Spirit, I began to partake of the heavenly fruit basket. Taking hold of the fruit of love, I would swallow, internalize the love of God and imagine the Holy Spirit pouring His love into my heart.

Next, I would take up a large portion of joy and swallow it whole, laughing as I did so, followed by peace, a most delicious fruit, smooth and quieting in His love, a rest with a great sense of protection.

Longsuffering is like a rubber band that stretches through time, always giving more opportunities for discovery rather than forcing answers. When partaken, frustration and impatience dissolve.

Kindness is greatness along with the receiving of His mercy and grace as it abounds inside. It then flows most freely to all outside.

Goodness is awesome. It is God. He is good, for His mercy endures forever. God abounds in goodness and truth and when this fruit is eaten, wholeness comes in place of fragmentation. Pieces become whole and fractures mend.

Faithfulness is our God. As I feed on His faithfulness, all fretting, worry and anxiety flee. In the place of my fears, I feel an over-whelming conviction of God's great ability and willingness to perform all His promises. Praise leaves my lips.

Gentleness. Such tenderness softens my hard exterior, my battle-fatigued soul and the wounds from the house of my friends, as He gently draws me to Himself again in love.

Self-control. Who would have thought that self-control would be a fruit and not an act of will? It is easy to eat self-control, experience His self-control and rest there in His love. Still, as with all the fruits of the Spirit, it is not a matter of my will but His will. He wills and works in me for His good pleasure. The fruit of the Spirit is our inheritance and exists for our enjoyment before we employ it.

Core Scriptures:
Hebrews 6:19–20; 2 Peter 1:2–4; 2 Corinthians 5:7; Luke 10:23–24;
1 Peter 1:10–12; 2 Corinthians 5:16; 1 Corinthians 3:1–4;
Galatians 5:16–26

59

"NO" IN THE NATURAL IS "YES" IN THE SPIRITUAL

A world awaits you, one that you have barely touched, where the word of God is alive and the voice of God fills the atmosphere.

It is the world of the Spirit, a place where you are given eyes to see. We see by faith, and faith comes by hearing, and hearing by the word of God. All journeys in the kingdom begin with a promise and the promise, the nod of God, will set you on a journey to perform the promise. Later, you become the promise.

Before that, you try to perform with the abilities you possess but those gifts and talents are not the same as the Holy Spirit. So, denial is our first experience; but we are strong people. We don't take "No" for an answer easily. The devil is not going to stop the work of God, so we try again and again and again.

The children of the promise come from a barren womb. The children of the flesh persecute the children of promise, making their lives miserable. What we don't realize is that our denials are our invitations to enter into the presence behind the veil and become the promise. When God denied David the right to build God's temple in the natural world, David went further into the spiritual. He fellowshipped with God in the Spirit and saw the temple in heaven. When it came time to pass the torch to his son, Solomon, David gave him the plans for the temple that he had designed while the hand of the Spirit was upon him.

The invitation to enter more fully into the promise was not given by the completion of the promise, but in the temporary denial of it. If it were otherwise, we would build through our gifts and talents alone.

Take a promise you have heard sometime before in your life and enter into it behind the veil, where hope awaits further exploration. Enter into His presence and then bring the promise before you. Feel the Holy Spirit begin to bring you up into the word and the expanse of that word.

It is uncanny how God's promises are not limited by the current status of the earth. They are not limited by our success or failure and they never will be because they originate from God and return to Him.

I have so struggled with this truth, because I am no stranger to God's promises or to denial—and I live in two worlds. We are all familiar with one world (earth). The other is the world that Jesus has prepared for us. There, His word is living, expansive and beckons us to enter.

When I do, I see a world framed by the word of God, even framing and weaving together our identity and eternity. So I sit with the Lord wanting more than anything for His word to come to pass but, in the Spirit, I am taken to see, experience and enjoy the word beyond anything that I could have imagined.

Let me illustrate it this way.

Say I believe God will find a way to give me a hundred dollars to pay a bill. As I press Him for this help in prayer, suddenly I become aware of a promise, such as: He will abundantly supply all my needs according to His riches in glory, that through His grace, I will have abundance. Those are three scriptures woven together with an invitation to enter in, I forget I need a hundred dollars.

I enter into eternity (His promises to me). There I see wealth, abundance and His treasuries filled with snow, water and lighting. I see more than enough, so much so, that I can't write down my recollections fast enough. They are so vivid. This is awesome! I think, *I am not only going to get the hundred dollars. I have been promised millions.*

Core Scriptures:
Hebrews 12:18–29; Romans 10:17; Galatians 4:21–31; 1 Chronicles 28;
Hebrews 6:19–20; 11:3; Philippians 4:19; 2 Corinthians 12:9; 9:8;
Job 38:22

60

THE BARREN WOMB

When I let God take me beyond my immediate need (my temporal "light afflictions," the Bible calls them), I enter into much more than what I was looking for. The hundred dollars that I was seeking has become the promise of great wealth, resources and freedom. I see the invisible, not the visible. I experience eternity, not reality. This is what it means to receive God's promise.

What happens when I leave this time in the Spirit with the Lord?

I expect the Lord to give me one hundred dollars or more because, on earth, I need the hundred dollars more than the promises I have been given. I need my bread and water, not the word of God that has been spoken over me.

This demand of sight cripples my trust and I soon wonder, *What is the meaning of all this promise if there is not any small fulfillment of it?* I doubt myself, *What is wrong with me, I can't even make a simple promise come to pass?*

God places His greatest promises in barren wombs. He leaves them there until all natural ability to bring them to pass is exhausted.

To keep His wombs alive, He feeds them with faith, hope and love in Himself (not from the world). Flesh looks at a barren womb and says, "You can't even have a baby and you think you're the mother of multitude?" Or flesh boasts saying, "You're barren. I have all these children. Therefore I am loved and you are not." In the face of accusations and fears, your soul shuts down and grief can take over. Even more, you may no longer be willing to fellowship with God behind the veil because your circumstances mock you.

But if you, like me, find your way back to God, in need, desire or by accident, you will find yourself in the Spirit again.

In the Spirit, God gives life to your dead places and calls things into being. Caught up in the Spirit, you enter in and before you know it, you are living and experiencing the promises again! Your natural reasoning warns, "Don't trust this. You'll be disappointed," or "Make sure you get it down right. Don't make mistakes like last time so that the promises will be fulfilled this time."

Distrust in God and relying on works are fleshly responses to the Spirit. Both are ways of maintaining control but neither will bring completion. You have to let go and trust God.

Letting go of my entire list of promises and outcomes was a huge prerequisite for my entering into the presence behind the veil. All those hundred-dollar prayers that led to million-dollar revelations left me fragmented, broken, bruised and breached.

I was just where God wanted me. I was ruined.

I had no more confidence in my flesh or strength to try again. I just needed to deal with my bitterness and ask the tough questions, such as "Where were you?" Then, I could encounter God like Job and Habakkuk and see that my reasoning had become my righteousness, leaving me to repent in dust and ashes. It sounds easy and it is, after it happens. Arriving at that point, still, is awful, because we can't see our pride, fear, arrogance and accusations against God.

Bitterness is failed expectation. It is failed grace and, as Christians, we can be full of it. Bitterness prevents us from entering into our freedom. (Here God is trying to bring us into Himself but we are sitting outside the party because we have never been given a goat to enjoy with our friends!) We have worked and received nothing. We feel forsaken and angry.

Good. Time to get honest. Ask the hard questions and wait for His answer—for an honest heart never goes unrewarded.

Core Scriptures:
Isaiah 54:1; Genesis 11:30; 25:21; 29:31; 1 Samuel 1:2; Luke 1:7;
Romans 4:17; Job 32:2; 42:5–6; Luke 15:29

61

OUR MINDS STAYED ON HIM

In the late 1970s, early on in my pilgrimage, I discovered a little book written by a seventeenth-century French monk known as Brother Lawrence titled, *The Practice of the Presence of God*. He was only a cook in the monastery but he developed such an abiding presence of God that many sought his counsel on developing a greater awareness of God's presence.

I have read this book many times over the last thirty years, and it still challenges and thrills my heart. Brother Lawrence believed and practiced the presence of God always by "staying" his mind on the Lord. He was always considering, aware of, and including the Lord in everything he did.

All of us can practice "staying our minds on Him." This is the first step toward intimacy and ultimate residency in the New Jerusalem. Having discovered the goodness of the Lord, we should desire, as babes, the milk of the word by reading the Bible in order to internalize it. We should fellowship with God rather than simply try to obey Him. It may be hard at first, since we are such doers.

Begin with your imagination as you read and pray. As you see the words, try to imagine what they might look like in heaven. Entering into the presence behind the veil is more than a series of steps. It is also an awareness of each place attained. Hold your mind, which, according to Isaiah 26:3, is your imagination, on the Lord in the scripture you have read or the message you've heard.

Do this and you will experience revelation throughout the day. The "holding of your mind" is the staying —which means, "to prop, lean upon or take hold of." When we practice this we are "occupying the place that has been prepared for us."

The Father does not speak accidentally but with the purpose of implanting His seed in us so that we may partake of His divine nature. This is organic, not mechanical. You can't hasten the gestation.

Instead, enjoy the word. Love His presence and wait for His Spirit to come and settle down upon you. God is not in a hurry. He is the best meal we will ever enjoy. So we should savor every encounter, returning often to the moment and memory.

I understood this but couldn't do this continually since I had such fear in my soul. I would soon be frightened out of fellowship and back into work of some sort for the Lord. I have aborted more words from heaven than I can even remember because I understood revelation but did not understand gestation. So I would force words into this earthly realm that had not matured in my spirit.

I was ashamed of this. But all things work for good. Our souls must run when they must run or control is the only other choice.

As trust is the fruit of love, control is the fruit of fear. The love of God gave us Christ and, now, our lives are hidden in Christ. You can imagine my surprise when I discovered that every word ever spoken to me was alive in heaven, awaiting my habitation. Our inheritance is in Christ. Therefore, it cannot be lost. We may depart, waste and even deny the Lord and His promises but the moment we return, all that has ever been given to us in Christ remains ours. It has not diminished. It has only increased in His presence.

As you set your mind on the Lord, you will develop trust, experience more and everything will be backed up on heaven's hard drive where the Holy Spirit can, at any moment, access it and recalibrate our frail lives into eternity.

Nothing is wasted in heaven.

Core Scriptures:
Isaiah 26:3; 1 Peter 2:1–3; John 14:2–3; 2 Peter 1:2–4; 1 Peter 1:3–5

62

PRAISE HIM

Praise begins as a sacrifice of our lips in giving thanks to His name; and thanksgiving is the way we enter His gates.

For many years, I advised friends to praise first, and then complain. Honesty is rewarded but not without faith. Faith is challenged every day because it is our assurance of the promises we have been given. The pressure we feel is meant to have us let go of these promises and our faith.

Praise establishes for us who God is. It shifts our feelings from helplessness to strength and from abandonment to certainty in His victory. Praise is prophetic because it begins in what we know about God and will continue into the hope of the future behind the veil. Like Moses on the other side of the Red Sea, praise starts with that victory and continues into the conquest of the entire promised land.

But less than two years later, as Israel faced the giants of the land, they retreated into apathy and rebellion against God. Why? They had forgotten their praise.

Practicing the presence of God demands praise to establish His glory—especially when we are at war. The ominous threats of our adversary, along with his shouts of accusations and condemnations, will paralyze the most seasoned warrior. The devil shouts. God whispers. The devil shouts because he has no authority. Our Jesus whispers because He has all authority. Praise shuts the mouth of our adversary and amplifies the still, small voice of our Father into the thunderous sound of heaven!

Praise does not have to be religious but it should be real.

Thanking God is the basis of our sanity, just as glorifying God is. Although God does not need our praise, we are the ones who need to praise God. Otherwise, our hearts become darkened and our thoughts become futile.

We sink into despair or delusion because we move away from Eternal Life. Granted, the circumstances of our lives and the subtle (and not so subtle) accusations will sow doubt into our hearts, causing us to wonder or ask, *What good will this do? Surely if God was going to deliver me, He would have. He must be angry or neglectful.*

All of these emotional thoughts of doubt toward God's goodness and His faithfulness are our training for reigning. Praise takes hold of these doubt-filled, self-pitying moments and shifts the atmosphere back toward our overcoming Lord, who loves us continually, is pleased with our smallest moments of faith and can't wait to love on us at our first movement toward Him.

Praise is your responsibility—not someone else's. No one can praise for you, and no one else's praise can carry you. Sure, there are times when it's hot and praise is bursting forth in everyone and from everyone, but that's easy. What about when you are alone and have been thinking of failure and desertion? When you're out of money and the rent is due?

This is when praise counts; it activates faith and changes atmospheres. When Job lost all his possessions and all his children, he tore his robe, shaved his head, fell on the ground and worshipped. When Israel was surrounded by three nations without any possible deliverance, the Israelites went out singing, "The Lord is good, for His mercy endures forever." When Paul and Silas found themselves in a Macedonian jail, their backs bloody and their feet in stocks, the prisoners around them heard them praying and singing hymns to God.

God heard, too.

He sent the earthquake that shook open the doors, unlocked the chains and brought salvation to everyone in the prison that night. The Lord heard Israel, too. He caused the nations gathered against Israel to rise up and kill each other. The Lord restored to Job twice what he had lost.

So when you have lost your balance, praise until you can stand.

Core Scriptures:
Hebrews 13:15; Psalm 100:4; Romans 1:21-22; Exodus 15:1–21;
Psalm 106:10–13, 24–26; 1 Kings 19:11–13; Job 1:20–2; Acts 16:25–26;
2 Chronicles 20:20–23

63

PRAY UNTIL YOU FEEL THE LORD

I pray until I feel something. Because I am an emotional creature made in His likeness, I am made to feel the presence of God.

Learning to feel the presence of God may take a bit of time but it really isn't that hard. The presence of the Lord is righteousness, peace, and joy in the Holy Spirit. Righteousness feels like "it's all right," that things are well and will be well. Righteousness feels like total acceptance and validation, being loved and well cared for.

It is a sense of justice and rightness surrounding you, even deliverance and victory. Any of these feelings, as we pray, is an indication of the Holy Spirit's close proximity and comfort. When you feel the littlest of these emotions, lean into them and agree with the Lord that He is there for you.

Peace feels like a spa on a cold winter night or like a fireplace, a cup of hot chocolate in your hand and safety as you sit indoors while outside it rains, hails or snows. Peace feels like permission to move forward. It is calm, gentle and does not stir itself up.

Like the glassy sea before the throne of God, peace sits content, undisturbed, yet forcefully protecting what it surrounds. When you feel His peace, lean into it. Acknowledge it and enjoy. It is well with your soul.

Joy feels like joy! Joy is a strength that defies odds and courage that laughs at the threat of death. Joy is faith's companion and freedom's sound. Joy is the atmosphere of heaven, expectant and pregnant with celebration of the Lamb and His overcoming victory.

Joy doesn't know defeat because there is always another day and more time for God to prove His greatness and increase your net worth. Yes. Joy is the flag flown high from the castle of my heart when the king is in residence here. When you feel joy, lean into it and rejoice.

My first destination in prayer is to pray until I sense the Lord and feel His presence.

Today, when I come up to sit with Jesus on His throne, I wait for the flush of joy, peace and righteousness to take hold of my soul (so that it can become quiet in His love and rest). I continue praising and glorifying His name until I feel the truth of my words. In this, I am recalibrating my soul to submit to the Spirit of God and His kingdom.

I pray until the Greater One in me has overcome all my fears. I pray until I have the victory inside and joy is alive within me. Again, what am I doing? I am recalibrating my soul with my spirit. I am adjusting the atmosphere in my interior to match the atmosphere in heaven. I am settling into my Father's arms, resting my head in His bosom or I am running and playing with Jesus on heaven's grassy hills.

As feelings come, let your imagination take hold of them. Look at them with your spiritual sight. See outcomes that are favorable without spending any time on figuring anything out. Knowing He is able and that His power is moving towards you for victory, shifts confidence and trust. There is no need to know how He is going to do any of it.

Imagination is hope alive. Watching the Lord move or dance is also hope alive. Hope is the image needed to give faith substance. Again, it is not necessary to see how it will turn out. Just seeing the Lord's active involvement is enough.

We pray until we feel, until we see, until we know. Then we can do any business we need to transact with the Father – even though, most of the time, it has already been swallowed up in victory.

Core Scriptures:
Romans 14:17; Isaiah 55:12; 1 John 4:4; Romans 8:5

64

JUDGE HIM FAITHFUL

"**S**ing, O barren, You who have not borne! Break forth into singing, and cry aloud, You who have not labored with child! For more are the children of the desolate than the children of the married woman," says the Lord. (Isaiah 54:1)

Sarah had to judge God faithful even though, in experience, it appeared He had been unfaithful. She had to let go of the past and take hold of His presence. She had to judge Him faithful who had promised.

Sarah was the married woman, though barren. Unable to bear a child on her own, she gave Hagar to Abraham but, as soon as Hagar conceived, she despised Sarah and belittled her because Hagar had accomplished what Sarah could not. Sarah's anger turned against Abraham and he gave Hagar into Sarah's hands to do with as she pleased. Sarah treated Hagar harshly, making her life miserable, until Hagar could take no more and fled for home. Off to Egypt she went but the Angel of the Lord found her, prophesied over her child and instructed her to return and submit to Sarah.

Hagar called the Lord "You-Are-the-God-Who-Sees, for she said, 'Have I also here seen Him who sees me?'" (Genesis 16:13)

The wonders of our God are incredible. While Sarah stewed, fuming over this mess with Hagar and the inadequacy she felt and while Abraham was perplexed and wondered what in the world was happening, Hagar was having an encounter with the Lord. He spoke promise into Hagar and Ishmael.

Don't ever think that events in the present have ruined the future. God is always speaking into all things and redeeming all things to Himself. He is always in front, behind and in the middle of all decisions and consequences, redeeming anyone and anything that will listen and turn toward Him. That is the promise in Isaiah 6 about hearing, seeing, understanding and *turning* toward Him to be healed.

Fast-forward thirteen years. The Angel of the Lord is outside Sarah's tent talking again to Abraham, promising that he would return again next year and that Sarah would have a son. Remember. Sarah was the married woman who was barren. She was full of promise but was unable to perform, having only bitter memories of trying to work out this promise herself:

> Sarah laughed within herself, saying "After I have grown old, shall I have pleasure, my lord being old also?" And the Lord said to Abraham, "Why did Sarah laugh, saying, 'Shall I surely bear a child, since I am old?' Is anything too hard for the Lord? At the appointed time, I will return to you according to the time of life and Sarah shall have a son." But Sarah denied it, saying "I did not laugh," for she was afraid and he said, "No, but you did laugh!" (Genesis 18:12–15)

The Lord didn't get hung up on Sarah lying to Him. He stated that the promise was His to perform. He spoke to Abraham, demonstrating the covenant. Now, Sarah, the married woman, what was she going to do?

Does she deny the Lord because of past experiences? Does she try to help the Lord because of her inability? Does she control her diet or exercise?

No. She judged Him faithful. She went on rejoicing and received strength to conceive, trusting that He was able to perform His promise.

A few weeks later, as they were entering into the kingdom of Abimelech, when Abraham told her not to tell anyone they were married but, rather, were brother and sister, did that stop the Lord from declaring to Abimelech, "You're a dead man because the woman you have is married?"

No. The Lord defended the covenant. He defended Sarah and brought her out in dignity and grace. Sarah broke out in song, shouting aloud, "Nothing is too difficult for *you!*"

Laughter is a sign of disconnection from the self and reconnection with God and His ability. Laughter gave Sarah the strength to conceive!

Core Scriptures:
Isaiah 54:1; Genesis 16; Isaiah 6:10; Genesis 18:12–15; 20

65

HE SINGS OVER YOU

Did you know that the Lord joins our worship of the Father in our midst while He sings over our rejoicing? He does.

Jesus delights so much in what the Father has done in revealing Himself to babes and His drawing men to Himself, that once, while on earth, Jesus began twirling around, rejoicing in His spirit that the Lord had done this very thing. The disciples had been impressed with their prowess in ministry, even exorcising demons in Jesus' name, but Jesus directed their joy toward their identity in heaven, even their names written in the Lamb's book of life. They were delighted in power, He was delighted in privilege.

Being in the Spirit behind the veil has revealed such a different world than the one in which I work.

Jesus is not ashamed to be called our brother and sings praises with us to the Father. The phrase, "Jesus dwells in the midst of us," is more than some cliché. It is truth, a living truth that you can experience and live. We can live in and live from Jesus' word. Everything in the Bible is truth that we can live in and live from, all through Jesus.

Abiding in Christ takes us to a place where we encounter the resurrected Christ—glorious, victorious, overcoming, and triumphant. We become all of these wonderful and positional truths of Christ as we behold Him in His glory.

The door that opened to me and allowed me to live there was Christ—His death, burial and resurrection—all which took place for my sake. Believing in Him, God granted me salvation and a door of entrance.

Still, I thought my time in heaven, in His presence, was to bring *heaven to earth* and to shift all things I saw into the truth of heaven. That will happen but not thanks to my efforts, talents, zeal, integrity, honesty, you name it. I can't save anyone including myself.

So my efforts fail. My vision becomes confusion and I ask, "Why show me all this? Why promise me all this?" Answer: that the Lord may gain entrance into my life. To be in union with my life. To impart His divine nature in my life. To give me an anchor for my soul. To bring me into the presence behind the veil. That is why He gives His glorious promises to you and me.

When I was caught up and given a place to sit, I realized that I had been receiving this place in God for many years. Rejoicing, singing, laughing and playing—there seems no end to the wonder of His love.

The Lord sings over us. He sings songs of deliverance and songs of rejoicing. He dances and twirls all around. Now I don't see all these things with my natural eyes. I see His voice and, in His voice, I see Jesus.

The voice of the Lord is a manifestation of Jesus. Whether you are in a church service or all alone, when the Lord speaks, He has come. Hearing His voice brings faith and gives life. It awakens hope, quiets us in His love and, if you are willing, brings you into His presence, His heart, and further into His promises for you.

Reconciling heaven with the day in which I am living is not always easy. Limited time and resources apply pressures that grow quickly and, without knowing it, I find myself toiling again. Like Martha, I become distracted by too much servitude. I become accusing and controlling of the Lord and those around me.

That's when I hear Him come in the cool of the day. "Steve," He calls. "Come away with Me. Let us run together." For years I might join Him in His little escapades, hoping that at the end, we would deal with the really important stuff.

What I found was that *this* was the really important stuff.

Core Scriptures:
Hebrews 2:12; Zephaniah 3:17; Luke 10:21; Hebrews 10:20; Romans 10:17;
Luke 10:28–42

66

JOY: THE STRENGTH OF PATIENCE AND THE DOOR OF FAITH

"Why can't you be joyful? What is keeping you from joy?" I asked myself out loud. "Well, I have all these promises that have not been fulfilled. How do I reconcile that?" This is how: by judging God as faithful and, then, letting go of my disbelief, grief and my refusal to be comforted.

The natural world we live in is not our home nor will all promises be fulfilled here. In fact, the Bible teaches us that if you want to be miserable or to be pitied, then put your hope in Christ for this life alone: "If in this life only we have hope in Christ, we are of all men the most pitiable" (1 Corinthians 15:19)

The power of His presence, promises, faith, hope and love allow us to live in conflicting circumstances and impossible situations while living freely and victoriously in His presence and promise. Faith, hope and love are not dependent on our circumstances. They give access to eternity now in the presence of He who gives life to the dead and calls new life into being.

Living here in His word, without the demand of flesh, rests the soul. All of us have had moments of His great peace, that unexplainable peace that surrounds and seems to guard our souls. This is the reason for casting our cares on Him and for letting go of our fears and worries through prayer, supplication, and thanksgiving. We are sons and daughters who have been given all things in Christ, and even though we may struggle in this life to reconcile everything, the Lord does not.

It does not bother Him that you have not realized your dream nor does it make you less desirable that you are struggling to hold your faith. The value you have placed in Him, by hearing His voice and receiving His words of eternal life, gives Him great delight. The fact that you continue, despite the struggles and difficult situations you face, secures you in His compassion. He is filled with pleasure as you choose Him and His word.

The part I never understood was that I could fellowship with Him *now* in the promise, in His presence, and enjoy the fulfillment of eternity now. With joy, we draw water from the wells of salvation, and with joy we endure the cross and despise the shame. Joy is strength!

Intentionally laughing out loud is a point of contact for me. I laugh because it is funny how so much continues to struggle against His rule and against my soul. I laugh because I am funny in my anxiety and need for control. I laugh because He is good, and His mercy endures forever. I laugh because I know the One whom I have entrusted with all things.

I know I cannot do anything without Him. Nothing is too difficult for the Lord. So, in His love for me, I laugh at my circumstances and my anxious ways. His rejoicing over me is faith. (At least it is a door into faith.) Here in His presence, I hear His voice again singing over me, confident in what Jesus has accomplished.

I hear the Father say, "You are my son whom I greatly love. I highly favor you. You bring me much pleasure." What I want to say in my natural mind is, "Are you talking to me?" But I know better now. He is talking to me in His Son Jesus. All this is mine, no matter what. Whether I fall on my face or climb Mount Everest, I am His son, greatly loved and highly favored and I bring much pleasure to my Father.

So joy strengthens my patience and opens the door again for my faith. Miracles and all I need are provided for me in Christ according to His riches in glory. I experience eternity now—whether I see it or not.

Core Scriptures:
Jeremiah 31:15–17; 1 Corinthians 15:19; Philippians 4:6–7; Isaiah 12:3;
Hebrews 12:1–2

67

THE PROMISE REMAINS

Promise secures presence and presence increases promise. The married woman might be barren now in the kingdom but being married with promise is more wonderful than being fruitful without covenant.

Promises are eternal. They are the hope—sure and steadfast—that enters the presence behind the veil. They are the confession of our hope when we fellowship in that presence. Even if we give up on His promises, they remain in place, for Jesus cannot deny Himself.

Presence and promise are union in the Spirit, because here truth meets life. The promises are true, and the Spirit is life. What happened to me so supernaturally was a culmination on a large part of what had been happening over and over and over again when I entered His presence.

The dramatic jump came out of promotion and death of self, but it wouldn't have happened if the Lord had not prepared me. He prepared me by giving me promises over and over and over again. He prepared me by bringing me into His presence over and over and over again. He prepared me by allowing me to live in two worlds.

This built a capacity for God to dwell in me and me in Him. For many years, I had preached that the Holy Spirit is so optimistic about your life that, if you spend any time with Him, you will become convinced that you are living again, and that what He says is real.

When you go from His presence and attempt again to accomplish what He is saying, it may be just as before. You may still find yourself discouraged and frustrated at your inability to produce results but the Holy Spirit is not bothered by that because we are saved in hope and hope that is seen is not hope. The Holy Spirit communicates patience and He groans in our spirits in prayer, causing recalibration with eternity.

God's promises are the blueprints of heaven. They are the inheritance given, the "lines that fall in pleasant places," as David said.

So over and over and over again we come, we fellowship, experience, hear, live and we exist in Him. God's promises observed are the place of habitation for God in the Spirit and for us in Christ. The Holy Spirit fills the house. He awakens our spirits to His presence and the truth of His promises and here we are, holding fast to the confession of our hope in His presence.

It is amazing that we have been given unlimited access, unlimited time and unlimited views. If we want, we can live here. I did and then I didn't. Circumstances or trouble, pain, gain or fear—something would always move me from this truth into my present reality and wham-o, I would go back to striving, retreating or doubting. I would lose abiding in His presence.

Coming up and abiding with God is an event, similar to moving to your favorite vacation spot or dream house. You have visited there often but now it is yours because you have purchased it! You are a property owner at the invitation of the One who owns it all—God.

He called me into heaven and I sat in His throne, laughing at my former antics. I knew the place well but somehow, now, I stayed without being tossed to and fro.

Core Scriptures:
Isaiah 54:1–8; Hebrews 6:19–20; 2 Timothy 2:13; Romans 4:17; 8:24;
Psalm 16:5–6

68

RESTING IN HIS LOVE

Resting in His love is like sitting in a warm room with your spouse while soft music plays, filling the air with security and hope.

His love fills heaven. There, His love fills our hearts where the Father and Jesus have come to abide. The Holy Spirit pours out liquid love into every chamber of our hearts.

When I entered into His rest, I was amazed at how heaven is so peaceful and quiet, despite the sounds of thunder and God's voice. In the center of God is completeness like nothing we have known but we will know it in His complete abiding in us.

When I was called to dwell in heaven, I sat with the Father in Jesus, laughing and laughing. Joy filled my soul and all anxiety, frustration and strife left. This place was so awesome in the Lord. After having lived years in His word—contending, doing, striving, helping and whatever else I convinced myself was necessary—now I was resting.

Soon after the October 2011 experience, Cammy saw the change during a Wednesday night baptismal service. Things were not as they might have been. She thought to herself,

Steve is going to get really uptight over this. I wish I didn't have to be around as he fusses over it. To her surprise, I laughed, worshipped and had one of the best baptisms—because I could sincerely touch the people being baptized with joy and expectancy of what the Lord was doing in them. The circumstances had not wrecked my faith or challenged my position. I was in heaven, laughing at myself.

Cammy said later, "I really knew that the Lord had worked within you when I witnessed how you responded to what normally would have cost you your peace and sent you into fear and frustration. This time, it didn't. In fact, if anything, it propelled you into His presence." That is the joy of heaven.

We become fearful when we live as a servant with a list of demands to be accomplished by a certain time in a certain way. It is maddening to be a servant full of bondage and fear. Jesus' complete work, whether received or rejected, is not threatened.

Jesus said that our sanctification from the world, the flesh and the devil, was through His word and in His presence, love and glory. Now, I am learning to live here without demanding the flesh to perform tasks. I am no longer overwhelmed when the flesh persecutes the Spirit. I am living in freedom.

Promises are eternal and so are His love, His presence, and His glory. All continue uninterrupted while confusion and hell breaks forth around us. We can enter into the presence behind the veil through the promises given (our hope), through the blood that has redeemed us (our purchased price) and through Jesus' new and living way.

We can experience peace beyond understanding, resting in His love.

Core Scriptures:
Romans 5:5; Hebrews 4:9–11; Galatians 4:25–31; John 14:23; Revelation 21:2; John 17:14–26; Hebrews 10:19–23

69

SHOW ME YOUR GLORY

After having obtained a promise from the Lord that He would show Moses His way and that His presence would go with the Israelites, Moses asked to see the glory of God.

Now, the promise of His way and presence resolved for Moses the potential dilemma of Israel going into the Promised Land led by an angel but without God's presence. Moses, however, needed another experience in the glory, more than the burning bush or the ten miracles and plagues. He needed something more than dining with the Lord, Aaron, and the seventy elders on the mountain of God, even something more than the forty days he spent in the cloud of God.

Moses had talked with God face-to-face in his tent (which he set outside the camp during the days that followed the incident of the golden calf). Moses had interceded and obtained the promise of His presence but still he asked, "Please, show me Your glory." (Exodus 33:18)

> Then He said, "I will make all My goodness pass before you and I will proclaim the name of the Lord before you. I will be gracious to whom I will be gracious, and I will have compassion on

whom I will have compassion." But He said, "You cannot see My face for no man shall see Me and live.'" (Exodus 33:19–20)

Moses was about to experience God in totality, not a portion or toned-down version. The Lord had already revealed Himself face-to-face to Moses but He had only offered a limited view. So now as He fully appeared, all of God in a moment of time, the Lord set Moses in the cleft of the rock, placed His hand over him as He passed by and proclaimed the name of the Lord. All His goodness passed by and Moses saw the backside of God as He lifted His hand.

There is so much more of God that we have yet to experience and see. He is our reward when we diligently seek Him. Still, something happens when you see God's glory at any level, whether it's a beautiful sunset declaring the glory of the Lord or an awesome worship service where we see the effects of God's glory in us.

An encounter with Jesus in His word reveals the glory of God in the face of Jesus, which brings transformation. Entering into that glory, we are given the opportunity to see, open the door and see more. And we are transformed.

This was what Moses was asking for when he said, "Please show me Your glory."

The Lord said, "I will make all my goodness pass before you, and I will proclaim the name of the Lord before you." Imagine what that would feel like?

Moses saw so much glory that his face shone when he came down from the mountain. Seeing this, the people became afraid and ran away. So Moses had to cover his face when he spoke with the people. Moses had seen the totality of God and knew of Christ's coming.

Christ came as a Son and we are His house. The glory of God seen in the face of Jesus Christ far outshines the glory that the people saw in Moses' face. Moses was the giver of the law but the ministry of the Spirit is more glorious. We are invited to know the Lord beyond what anyone could ever know from the law. Christ has taken the veil away so we can enter into the presence behind the veil.

Glory transforms us. It establishes us and determines everything we do. Moses knew he needed a whole new experience in the glory of God, beyond what he had known, if he was going to bring Israel into the Promised Land with the Lord. God knew this, too.

Please, show me Your glory.

Core Scriptures:
Exodus 33:12–23; 34:5–7; 2 Corinthians 4:6; Exodus 34:29–35; Hebrews
3:1–6; 2 Corinthians 3:7–18

70

AUTHORITY IS ACCESS

Moses built the tabernacle in the wilderness according to the pattern he had received from the Lord in His presence. Now, as Israel was about to enter into the Promised Land, Miriam and Aaron had grown envious of Moses, finding fault with his wife because she was an Ethiopian.

God was furious. Descending in a cloud, He stood at the doorway of the tabernacle and commanded Miriam, Aaron and Moses to come. There, the Lord declared that the place Moses held in His presence was like no one else's before Him. What were Aaron and Miriam thinking to speak against Moses?

> Then He said, "Hear now My words: if there is a prophet among you, I, the Lord, make Myself known to him in a vision; I speak to him in a dream.
>
> Not so with My servant Moses; he is faithful in all My house. I speak with him face to face, even plainly, and not in dark sayings; and he sees the form of the Lord.
>
> Why then were you not afraid to speak against My servant Moses?" (Numbers 12:6–8)

God defines authority as access. He defended Moses by declaring the access He had given Moses to Himself compared to other prophets.

God believes that He is God and the greatest privilege man can know is access to Himself. Moses did not see the glory of God in a sunset, in a vision or a dream. He saw God face-to-face and spoke with God as a man speaking to his friend.

The cloud departed from above the tabernacle and suddenly Miriam became leprous. Aaron saw this and began pleading with Moses: "Oh, my lord! Please do not lay this sin on us, in which we have done foolishly and in which we have sinned." (Numbers 12:11) Their speaking against Moses turned into pleading with Moses.

God had put things in perspective. Moses knew the Lord face-to-face (in fact, his face had shone from the glory) and now Miriam was leprous. The Lord's anger had been aroused because these two people did not perceive the worth He had given Moses by the access He had granted him. They spoke against Moses because of the Ethiopian woman he married. Their prejudice and self-righteousness fueled their arrogance. They thought themselves equal to Moses because they had prophesied and the Lord had used them.

Being used by the Lord does not mean you have access to the Lord. It does not make you equal with anyone. Being used by the Lord must move you toward knowing the Lord yourself—until you have found the place prepared for you—and are known by Him there.

Jesus said that some seeking to enter the kingdom of heaven will be denied access. They will counter this denial by saying,

"Lord, Lord, have we not prophesied in Your name, cast out demons in Your name, and done many wonders in your name?" And I then will declare to them, "I never knew you; depart from Me, you who practice lawlessness!" (Matthew 7:22–23)

Luke's account of the story is:

"Lord, Lord, open for us." And He will answer and say to you, "I do not know you, where you are from,"

Then you will begin to say, "We ate and drank in Your presence, and You taught in our streets."

But He will say, "I tell you I do not know you, where you are from. Depart from Me, all you workers of iniquity." (Luke 13:25b-27)

It's all about being *known* by the Lord.

"Knowing" is the same Greek word for intimacy with your spouse, like when Joseph took Mary to be his wife after the angel assured him the child was God's.

And did not know her till she had brought forth her firstborn Son. And he called His name, Jesus. (Matthew 1:25).

Knowing is more than showing God. It is giving the Lord access to our hearts and gaining access to His heart. It is more than eating and being in His meetings. It is eating His flesh and drinking His blood, becoming His home.

Being known is everything.

Core Scriptures:
Exodus 25:8–9; Numbers 12:1–16; Matthew 7:21–23; Luke 13:24–27;
Matthew 1:25

71

FRIENDSHIP IS EVERYTHING

Authority is access and friendship is intimacy.

The greatest friend of God ever named was Abraham, the man who would sit and listen to God speak of things to come as though they had already happened. Although being privy to the greatest promises ever given to a man, Abraham died possessing only a grave site and His promised son, Isaac.

Abraham had personal prophecy about his children, their journey to Egypt and four hundred years of captivity before he even had a son. Abraham saw a city whose builder and architect was God and set out on a pilgrimage to find that city. Seeing it far-off, he was content to call himself a pilgrim and God was pleased to be his God.

Abraham offered up Isaac as a burnt offering and would have done so fully expecting Isaac to die if the Lord had not called for him to stop. That is how confident Abraham was in God. After that, the Lord spoke to Abraham about multiplication, blessings and his seed (Christ) possessing the gates of His enemies.

When Jesus spoke to the religious as they wrestled with His offer for freedom (through abiding in His word), He said, "your father Abraham rejoiced to see My day, and he saw it and was glad." (John 8:56)

Abraham was a friend of God because he would allow God to speak and would believe over and over and over again.

I have enjoyed great access to God's heart and I have heard many wonderful promises in His presence but it is only now that I have come into the rest of faith, where I allow the Lord to speak and show me things that do not yet exist, without rushing out to try to accomplish them. His presence and His promise are enough.

The Lord continues to speak of things to come with greater and greater expanse, allowing me to see more of Christ than I ever thought possible. I love letting the Father share His heart and intentions and purposes, knowing that I am not a servant being commanded but a friend. Trust has taken the place of fear and lust. Now, I can enter further in and further up into the heart of my Father.

Listening to His word, like Mary of Bethany who chose that good part, causes the heart of God to be ravished with one look of our eyes. The place that Jesus prepared for us was Himself through His death on the cross, burial and resurrection. Jesus has now become our dwelling place—His blood our confidence, His death our access, as we come boldly into the holiest of holies.

Sitting with Him, we are invited to enjoy Him, to laugh with Him and to listen to His voice. The voice of our Beloved leaps upon the mountains and skips upon the hills; it beckons us to come away with Him. This is our honor. It is our inheritance and our highest calling.

We are now friends of God as Jesus said because we know what He is doing. We are now privy to His conversation with the Father and the Father's conversation with Christ. These promises, those nods of God, are revealed to us by the Spirit.

We may die with as little as Abraham possessed—with more promises yet to be fulfilled than have been fulfilled—but as we die in faith and finally depart from this place, we will carry our friendship with God into eternity.

Knowing God and Jesus Christ, whom our Father sent, we will look upon the city that God has built and we will rejoice again and again and again. The Lord will wipe away every tear, all trauma and ridicule, barrenness and reproach, abandonment and loss—death will be no more.

Friendship is everything. Listening, loving, and turning to Him in His word is friendship with God.

Core Scriptures:
Romans 4:17; Genesis 25:7–10; 15:13–16; Hebrews 11:17–19; Genesis 22:1–19; John 8:56; Song of Solomon 4:9; 2:8–10; 1 Corinthians 2:9–10; Hebrews 11:10; Revelation 21:45

72

YOUR FRIEND IS SICK

"Your friend is sick." That's what Jesus heard when the messengers from Bethany arrived and told Him, "He whom You love is sick" (John 11:3b).

The Greek word "love" here is "*phileo*," which means to "be a friend to, be fond of, have affection for." Jesus' friend, Lazarus, was sick. Lazarus was the brother of Mary and Martha. They lived together in Bethany, just outside of Jerusalem.

Now, Jesus liked Lazarus. He liked Mary and Martha. He enjoyed their company and stayed at their house whenever ministry brought Him to Jerusalem. The temple (His Father's house) had been overtaken by pride, fear, envy and all that masquerades as holy, becoming only a tomb filled with dead bones.

Jesus didn't like the place. So, after ministering in the temple, He would retreat back to Bethany and rest at the home of Lazarus, Mary and Martha. Jesus enjoyed their fellowship and their company. They were His friends.

"When Jesus heard that Lazarus was sick He said 'This sickness is not unto death, but for the glory of God, that the Son of God may be glorified through it.'" (John 11:4) Jesus made a declaration of faith that the sickness was not unto death but for the glory of God. Then the scripture says, "Now Jesus loved Martha and her sister and Lazarus." (John 11:5) I believe this is inserted to let us know of His *agape* (love) of the family. The word "love" here is translated from the Greek "*agapao*," which means "to love."

What does all that have to do with "Your friend is sick?"

Jesus was directed by the Father to "stay two more days in the place He was." (John 11:6) Jesus could not move out of the will of the Father and His will was glory, not death—"...for the glory of God, that the Son of God may be glorified through it." Something much bigger was going on than a friend who was sick and needed to be healed.

God's affection may be delayed but not denied.

God takes care of His friends. He raised Lazarus from the dead, bringing their relationship into resurrection and life glory. Now, the chief priests (Jesus' rivals) sought not only to kill Jesus but plotted to put Lazarus to death also. Why? Because it was on account of Jesus' raising of Lazarus that many of the Jews believed in Jesus.

There's nothing like a friendship resurrected.

Six days before Passover, after a long day of confrontation in the temple with the Pharisees, Sadducees and lawyers, Jesus was again in the house of Lazarus, Mary and Martha. Jesus sat at the table with the resurrected Lazarus sitting with Him. Martha was serving when suddenly Mary came in and, taking a pound of very costly oil of spikenard (worth a year's salary), she anointed Jesus' feet, wiping them with her hair.

The whole house filled with the fragrance of the oil. This was the tipping point, not the confrontation with religious and political leaders that day—Jesus was well adept at that.

The tipping point that initiated the end was a meal together in friendship and unity, culminating with worship far beyond the natural setting. Mary had prepared this for the day of His burial, though I doubt Mary knew this consciously.

Here, as the house filled with the fragrance of the oil of worship, all of Jesus' natural companions and disciples, especially Judas, became outraged, demanding, "Why this waste?" The natural mind could not receive the ideas of the Spirit. Jesus defended Mary and her prophetic act, declaring that wherever this gospel is preached in the whole world, this act would be told as a memorial to her! After this meal, Judas left the house and arranged for his betrayal.

Nothing threatens religion like friendship resurrected.

Core Scriptures:
John 11; 12:1–11

73

THE TIPPING POINT

L azarus was not a disciple (he is not mentioned with the twelve or the seventy). He was Jesus' friend. Friendship with God began with Abraham. In the Bible, he is the most often quoted as being a friend of God.

What makes a friend? For God, it is believing in His word. It is faith but not faith striving to do, but rather, resting in what God said.

The scene of Mary and the oil was a tipping point for Judas. He could no longer walk with Jesus in fellowship, friendship and fragrance of worship. Judas could not cope with the absurdity of such waste just as the chief priests could not cope with the multitudes leaving religion in favor of friendship, especially resurrected friendship. Lazarus must go, too.

Nothing threatens religion more than friendship because it challenges religion's position and place. Friendship is not based on works but value. Friends do not try to get something from each other. They simply share values and joys, similar passions and delights.

Lazarus, Mary, and Martha had become Jesus' friends because they invited Him into their house, sat at His feet, listened to His words and fed Him. In the beginning, there was confusion and strife when

Martha became all worked up over the food preparation, accusing the Lord of not caring that her sister, Mary, had left her alone to serve. She even told Jesus what to do, "Tell her to help me."

I can see Jesus chuckling to Himself as He replied,

> "Martha, Martha, you are worried and troubled about many things. But one thing is needed, and Mary has chosen the good part, which will not be taken away from her." (Luke 10:41b–42)

It is funny how enjoying His presence and listening to His words were the good part.

Anyway, Martha probably settled down and went back into the kitchen or perhaps she sat down with Mary and listened to Jesus' words, too. Jesus liked this family because they made room for Him to sit, eat and share His heart.

When we value the Lord, we make a place in our hearts for Him to lodge. When we hear His word, we give Him a place inside our hearts to lodge and, when we sit still, we enter into His rest.

In October 1999, when I gave the Lord my little revival, another event happened a couple of weeks later that would become a memorial to me. The reason it became a memorial was not the event alone. Rather, it was because it was the "suddenly" of a series of decisions over the course of many years,

The day it came into full clarity, both my desire and struggle became a prayer. Here is what I wrote in my journal October 21, 1999:

Today in prayer, I came to realize my quest for God was putting a demand on God to show up and do [something]. Dear Father, I do not know if this is acceptable, but I want this to be a place of Your rest. I'm sorry to want You for something. May this house be a place of Your rest. Whatever You desire, whatever You wish, let us be that for You. You are so good and so kind, and I so want You. I won't try to take from You, get from You, or have from You. I don't know if I can do this, but I'm willing.

May this be a house where I don't put demands on You, where You can come and rest and be among Your people and do as You like—like Lazarus's house, a place of rest. It seems my striving to obtain and do results in flesh and struggle. I'm sorry; please forgive my selfish ambition. God, I love you. You are my friend. Please feel comfortable and rest here for a while.

I really didn't know if I could assume to become a place of His rest but I have come to find out I could. I am not only a place of His rest but also a place of fellowship, friendship and joy.

He had placed that prayer in me.

Core Scriptures:
2 Chronicles 20:17; Isaiah 41:8; James 2:23; John 11; 12:1–12: Luke 10:38–42

74

FRIENDSHIP AND ACCUSATION

 All friendships are tested, not by design but through the natural course of life. In Mary, Martha and Lazarus's case, it was the Lord's delay in coming to heal Lazarus that resulted in his untimely death. In Abraham's situation, it was the command to offer his son Isaac as a burnt offering on a mountain of God's choice.

Confusing? Yes. How do you reconcile a God who makes a promise and then wants it to be offered as a burnt offering; or a God who delights in your company but delays in your emergency? What's going on?

Hint. It is not God who is being stretched. It is us.

In Abraham's case, he had many years of walking with God to center him when God made the radical request, asking him to offer his son, Isaac, as a burnt offering. The book of Hebrews says that Abraham fully expected that the Lord would resurrect Isaac from the dead. Abraham had told the young men who had accompanied him and Isaac to remain at the base of Mount Moriah as he and Isaac went up to worship (Genesis 22:5). Abraham had resolved to follow the voice of the Lord fully, without entering into the confusion of human emotion.

Abraham in complete trust towards God, moved up the mountain with his son, Isaac, fully prepared to offer him as a burnt offering. He knew that resurrection would have to follow because God's promises in Isaac were not yet fulfilled.

Jesus made a similar decree about Lazarus, "This sickness is not unto death, but for the glory of God, that the Son of God may be glorified through it." (John 11:4b) Jesus then stayed two more days in the place He was. Jesus was walking in the Spirit as Abraham had and the voice of the Father held Him, not the circumstances of the moment or its emotions.

But nobody else knew.

The rest of His disciples were ignorant of the high stakes drama that was unfolding. After two days, Jesus said, "Let us go to Judea, again." The disciples probably thought, "You're crazy. They just tried to stone you there." Jesus, ever drawing men unto Himself, assured them that as long as they walked in His light, they would not stumble. He went on to say, "Our friend Lazarus sleeps, but I go that I may wake him up."

They had heard about Lazarus's sickness and thought that sleep meant he was recovering. Jesus, ever in faith and fellowship with the Father, held His place of faith and did not give death its final say. Jesus said to them plainly, "Lazarus is dead. And I am glad for your sakes that I was not there, that you may believe. Nevertheless let us go to him." (John 11:14–15)

Did the disciples understand? No. Thomas said to his fellow disciples, "Let us go that we may die with Him."

When Jesus arrived, the reception was not any better. First, Martha accused Jesus saying, "Lord, if You had been here, my brother would not have died." Now Lazarus is referred to as Martha's "brother," not Jesus' "friend." It was personal. Jesus had let her down. She accused Jesus of delay while acknowledging her faith in a future resurrection. Past and future—but what about now?

> Jesus said to her, "I am the resurrection and the life. He who believes in Me, though he may die, he shall live. And whoever lives and believes in Me shall never die. Do you believe this?"
>
> She said to Him, "Yes, Lord, I believe that You are the Christ, the Son of God, who is to come into the world." (John 11:25–27)

Mary came and said the same thing, "Lord, if You had been here, my brother would not have died."

I said the same thing a few years after I asked the Lord to make our house His house of rest. Why did You delay in answering my prayer? Why did You not come? If You had been here, death would not have entered.

Jesus had to walk out what Abraham walked out with his son, Isaac. He had to fear God.

Sounds strange?

But, as a man, Jesus had to fear God above human emotions or circumstantial events.

Core Scriptures:
John 11; Genesis 22; Hebrews 11:17-19

75

ASSUMPTIONS AND RIGHTS

Jesus stood with Mary at His feet, weeping uncontrollably. Jesus saw the Jews that had come with her, also weeping, and He groaned in His spirit and was troubled. His feelings of grief, loss and pain were in opposition to the word the Father had given Him (and which He spoke) more than four days before: "This sickness is not unto death, but for the glory of God, that the Son of God may be glorified through it" (John 11:4).

Jesus was in His own test. He was being tempted to succumb to natural human inclinations, either by leaving immediately to heal Lazarus out of friendship or by entering into all the unbelief, grief and accusation against Himself and God. Jesus loved Lazarus, just like Abraham loved Isaac. The Father proved that Jesus' love for Lazarus was submitted to Him, not in competition with Him.

As Jesus stood watching them weep, groaning in His spirit, He said,

"Where have you laid him?" They said to Him, "Lord, come and see."

Jesus wept.

Then the Jews said, "See how He loved him!"

And some of them said, "Could not this man, who opened the eyes of the blind, also have kept this man from dying?" (John 11:34–37)

This was a mess!

The whole group was caught up in love, loss, doubt and questions. This massive human pain was like an agitated ocean, a stormy sea. Violent waves crashed on top of Jesus as He approached the tomb. Jesus again groaned in Himself and said, "Take away the stone." Martha, ever practical, said, "Lord, by this time there is a stench, because he has been dead four days."

Jesus was not interested in viewing a dead Lazarus.

They rolled the stone away, and Jesus lifted up His eyes and said:

"Father, I thank You that you have heard Me. And I know that You always hear me, but because of the people who are standing by I said this, that they may believe that You sent Me."

Now when He had said these things, He cried with a loud voice, "Lazarus, come forth!"

And he who had died came out bound hand and foot with grave clothes, and his face was wrapped with a cloth. Jesus said to them, "Loose him, and let him go." (John 11:41–44)

Way to go, Jesus!

I have been in tons of meetings where many of us shouted, "Lazarus, come forth!" The truth is that there wasn't an ounce of faith that day in Mary, Martha and all the others for a resurrection. There was obedience but no faith. But Jesus was in fellowship with the Father and in agreement with His word.

What does all this mean?

Friendship with God is dangerous to the natural sentiments of man, often challenging our loyalties to God. Resurrection is always on God's mind but that usually requires natural death.

Elijah stayed with a woman and her son died. Elisha had earlier prayed for a barren woman to have a son and then he later died...but they were resurrected!

In the big picture, the church has grown sick and died, buried in the tomb of religion with the grief and sorrow of this world swirling around it. Jesus again has made intercession for us and declared, "This sickness is not unto death but for the glory of God that the Son of God may be glorified through it."

We are each working out our disappointments, failures, losses and accusations until the Lord makes His way to our tomb, commanding us to roll away the stone. We may protest, our common sense again taking hold, our sentiment trampled upon but we will obey.

Core Scriptures:
John 11; Matthew 17:17; Ezekiel 37:1–4

76

RESURRECTED FRIENDSHIP

When I was called up into His presence, I was like those who dream. My mouth was filled with laughter and my tongue with singing. The Lord has done a great thing! I saw that His word is truth. His love is continuous and faithful. I had passed through the fear of death into the experience of death and now rested in the resurrection of friendship.

I don't know how to explain it another way. The place of friendship, access and intimacy you share with the Lord is contested, challenged and perplexing until it is resurrected.

> We are hard pressed on every side, yet not crushed; we are perplexed, but not in despair; persecuted, but not forsaken; struck down, but not destroyed—always carrying in the body the dying of the Lord Jesus, that the life of Jesus also may be manifested in our body. For we who live are always delivered to death for Jesus' sake, that the life of Jesus also may be manifested in our mortal flesh. (2 Corinthians 4:8–11)

Friendship, fellowship, intimacy, the invitations of the Spirit and our own personal pursuits may sicken, wither, die and be resurrected. We are joined to the word we believe and the promises we have been given. Our soul life may experience ecstasy and bewilderment, grief and loss, and a sword that pierces our heart. The Son must call us forth like Lazarus and take away our grave clothes so we can wear the bride's garments.

But in these exchanges, something so wonderful, eternal—so real and surreal—happens. We pass from our enslavement in fear of death to our indifference to it.

Why do believers, of all people, live in such materialistic, sentimental affection? Because we somehow thought the Lord's visits to our house would mean only life and not death. Our fear of death binds, torments, and prevents us from knowing complete and total love. We had not agreed upon death but His death is our death. His resurrection is our resurrection.

A resurrected friendship cannot be shaken.

The last enemy to be defeated is death. We shall overcome the accuser of the brethren by the blood of the Lamb, the word of our testimony and because we do not love our lives unto the death. Our natural sentiment must yield to His eternal faithfulness.

Our accusations and claims, such as Martha's, "My brother would not have died if You had been here," and subtle accusations of "Where were You?" must be swallowed up in His resurrection and life.

When the Lord brought me into His glory, I was like those who dream. My captivity had been turned. I saw Jesus sitting at the right hand of the Father and He beckoned me to come and sit with Him on His throne. Because I was in the Spirit like John on the island of

Patmos, I moved forward with ease and assurance. This was my place now, in His presence and I never planned to leave.

Of course, I have been shaken and moved from this place since that first invitation; though, like the resurrected Lazarus, I have a seat at the table. I have keys to the house. Resurrected friendship is so attractive to those who are weary and tired, to anyone who has served the bondage of religion and zeal, who have sacrificed and obeyed only to be thwarted.

"Who's got your goat?" I often hear the Father say to me.

Like the elder brother in the parable of the Prodigal Son, we can serve without fellowship, obey without friendship and find ourselves lusting after a goat to make merry with our friends—when the whole kingdom and everything the Father has is ours.

Core Scriptures:
Psalm 126:1–3; James 1:16-17; Luke 2:34–35; Hebrews 2:14–15;1
Corinthians 15:54; Revelation 12:11; John 11:32; Revelation 1:10; 2
Corinthians 12:1–4; Luke 15:28–30

77

THE FRAGRANCE OF HIM

As we enter into this resurrection, we let go of our loss and forget the past. In resurrection, we behold the glory of God in the face of Jesus and become so attractive to God our Father and to the world which is lost in darkness. Light will shine and we will arise in the light of Christ as a light that shines in a dark place until the day dawns and the morning star rises in our hearts.

What a day that will be! The resurrected body of Christ. Bearing the image of the heavenly man.

Martha

In Lazarus' house, Martha prepared a meal during the closing hours of Jesus' ministry. She served without striving or attempting to control the Lord or her sister. She didn't micromanage the Lord through prayer. Instead, Jesus experienced friendship and fellowship through a lovingly prepared meal.

Lazarus

Lazarus sat at the table with Jesus, reigning in His rest, working by faith, not striving in the flesh. His friendship with Jesus was open. Lazarus' resurrection had made their friendship even more vibrant and fearless, full of love, joy and peace. He sat with Jesus in His rest.

Resurrected faith is friendship with God that is no longer based in outcomes. It is a friendship like Abraham's friendship with God. Your faith listens to the Father's declarations of fulfilled promise and it is enough. Faith is no longer calculated to bring a desired result but is instead fearless abandonment to the one you love. You can't kill what has already been resurrected.

Mary

In this environment of friendship, Mary's worship broke open extravagant love, poured forth like oil onto Jesus' feet. He is perfumed by our worship and our house is filled with its fragrance. He rises to sing with us and over us; we do not calculate the value of this worship. While the very rigid see this worship as wasteful or counterproductive, Christ loves it.

Who is this coming out of the wilderness, leaning on her beloved? It is us, the bride of Christ—our outward man weakened, leaning on Him.

As I lean on my Beloved, I find myself glorifying God for all He is and all He has done, convinced of His ability to perform all His promises. I am thankful for all the death that has yielded to His glory. In awe, I worship, laugh and rejoice because it is finished.

We are complete in Him; and He is love, our laughing, loving Lord.

Core Scriptures:
Philippians 3:7–14; 2 Corinthians 4:6; 2 Peter 1:19; John 12:1–19; Song of Solomon 8:5; 1 Corinthians 15:48–49; Colossians 1:27; 2 Corinthians 2:14–16

78

THE HIDDEN TREASURES OF DARKNESS

When Cyrus came to power as the king of Babylon, he came with a promise. He had been named and was prophesied by Isaiah hundreds of years before as the one who would unlock the treasures that had been taken by Nebuchadnezzar, who was yet to plunder the temple of God. The temple was to be rebuilt and Cyrus was to release what had been taken captive by disobedience.

There is no way any of us will not find treasures of God captured and taken from our land. We are God's field and His building, yet we are called to take heed with what we build. Discovering our loss is the beginning of being found. The discovery of captivity is the beginning of freedom. You can't be rescued if you don't know you're a captive.

Thank God, all our inheritance in Christ is unique and is reserved in heaven. The title deed of our incorruptible, undefiled and unfading inheritance is in heaven. We may discount the riches as worthless, selling ourselves to sin or sorrow, but we cannot lose our inheritance.

Yes. We can go back into bondage and eat with the pigs. When a man awakens to the Father's goodness and says, "I will return home to my Father's house," our welcome has been prepared for us and heaven rumbles with joy.

When I came up to abide in my Father's house, I was amazed to discover all the promises that God had given me were there in heaven and reserved for me. They had also increased in worth. The covenant that Jesus and the Father had made was between the two of them and we are in Christ. He is our propitiation and guarantee of the promises.

We may lose our place but He will never lose His place. He is the beginning and the end, the author and finisher, the initiator and completer. He is everything.

When Jonah came to himself in the belly of the great fish with seaweed wrapped around his head, he remembered the Lord. He prayed and his prayer was heard. Jonah began to sacrifice to the Lord with a voice of thanksgiving and set his heart to obey the Lord again. All the while he was inside the fish being slowly digested, then God intervened: "So the Lord spoke to the fish and the fish vomited Jonah onto dry land" (Jonah 2:10).

You are God's treasure and He will not be denied. You can refuse or forsake your own mercy, like Jonah almost did. But, when you look up towards heaven and call upon the Lord, you are saved. The promises made are still enforced in heaven and Cyrus will arise, if need be, to unlock it on earth.

Having been called up to live with the Father has changed my prayers. Instead of prayers of petition, I offer prayers of worship and total faith. I am no longer micromanaging God. Instead, I rest in His love. I know I still strive when I become afraid but, when I return to His presence, I am reminded of His faithfulness.

This is the power of turning to the Lord when we are lost. He knows where our treasure is and He knows where we have gotten ourselves. In short, He knows everything and is always thinking of our redemption. Turning into the Lord is the single most important thing to do when we are lost because once we have found Him, or have been found by Him, everything else is just details.

Core Scriptures:
Isaiah 44:28; 45:1–4; 1 Corinthians 3:9–17; 1 Peter 1:3–5; Luke 15:17–24; Revelation 1:11; Hebrews 12:1–2; 1 Thessalonians 5:24; Philippians 1:6; Jonah 2:7–10; Hebrews 6:19–20

79

ETERNITY NOW

Living in the presence behind the veil is the place of eternal hope. Every word spoken, every promise given and every purpose of God will be realized in time.

But eternity is now, so hope is alive with faith and love. The natural world doesn't define us nor does it understand us. God's word defines us. His presence assures us and His love surrounds us. Letting go of the natural restraints of unfulfilled promises and our past disappointments, allows us to step into eternity now, where God's promises are fulfilled.

Jesus lived in the now of faith and so was not moved by what He saw. Yes, He saw the Father and did what He saw the Father doing. He performed miracles, signs and wonders, but He also did not fight for His life, seek His own goals, command stones to be turned into bread or jump off temples.

His life was hidden in God and ours is hidden with Christ. So what do we do? We learn to live in His presence and enjoy God now. If every promise ever given, every nod to "go ahead and pick that up," was assured to come to pass, how would we live? We would live with confidence, even as patience perfects its work in us.

When I sit in my Father's presence in Christ, I sit in eternity *now*. I sit in complete love and am complete in Him *now*. God has given me all things that pertain to life and godliness *now*. I have partaken of His divine nature *now*. I am greatly loved, highly favored and bring much pleasure to my Father *now*.

I used to come in and out of this truth, mostly because I was still afraid. Before, I lived by sight. Now I live by faith. He is coming, that is for sure, but while I await His coming, I enjoy sitting in heaven with Him. I have become transformed in His sight. You and I will be changed internally before our exteriors catch up. Our dwelling place is in heaven; our city is in heaven; and we have been given unlimited access to enjoy eternity now.

All of the negatives we hear in this natural world should not stop us from hearing *"yes and amen"* in the spiritual world. Faith is the substance of things hoped for and the evidence of things not seen.

Sitting with Jesus in heavenly places and communing with my Father in His holy place has transformed me from a worm into a warrior; not because I can command all things to be seen, but because I am not moved by what I see. I am dangerous when I am not afraid. I am dangerous when I do not care if I win or lose, live or die. I am dangerous when I have been with Jesus and testify to what I have seen and heard.

I am so glad that, while my soul has gone in and out of agreement with God, the Father has reserved my inheritance in heaven. This is huge! You have not lost anything. Nothing that the Father has given you in Christ can ever be lost and nothing we do can undo what we have been given in Christ, because it is in Christ—not us.

You can run away from God for forty years or be locked up in hopelessness and fear for decades. You can be a slow learner or refuse Him when He speaks, but the moment you turn to the Lord, everything comes cascading into completeness in Christ.

Nothing is lost or stolen. Although we may be the worse for wear, everything will be swallowed up in His victory.

Core Scriptures:
Hebrews 7:19; John 5:19–21; John 18:36; 8:50; Luke 4:1–13; Colossians 1:1–4; 2 Peter 1:2–4; Revelation 12:11; Acts 4:13–20; Matthew 16:24–25

80

FURTHER CLOTHED

What will the end look like? Will it be a final battle of good versus evil, a nail-biting struggle with all the power of darkness pressing against the light, seeking to push it into oblivion?

No. It will be more like a big gulp of water as death is swallowed up in victory and mortality swallowed up by life. Another way to look at the end, whether apocalyptical or in dying to self, is as being "further clothed."

> For we who are in this tent groan, being burdened, not because we want to be unclothed, but further clothed, that mortality may be swallowed up by life. (2 Corinthians 5:4)

The Greek word here for "clothe" is to "sink into." The word, "unclothed" means to "sink out of." The Greek translation for "further clothed" means the "superimposition of sinking into."

Our tent is our mortal body. Paul said that if our tent is destroyed, we have an eternal habitation in heaven, created by God. According to Paul, we will slip out of our tents and into our heavenly habitation. When that happens, we will experience a "superimposition of sinking into." And, in that, mortality will be swallowed up by heavenly life. "Swallowed up" means to "drink down, to gulp entirely." Once we have successfully changed residences, death will be swallowed up in victory.

We all love to shop for clothes, or at least I do. Our wardrobe is earthly and temporary, yet we are preparing to live in heaven for eternity and will need new clothes. We begin with salvation, so rich and free. Jesus has become our propitiation (our sin offering) and we have become His righteousness. We enter into the presence behind the veil with promise and boldness given by His blood. We enter in and put on Christ's righteousness, peace and joy. We are going shopping, trying on Christ, learning to live in Christ—to wear Christ and to be renewed in His image.

At some point in time, taking off the old man and putting on the new man will be more like sinking into the new man and sinking out of the old man. Then, corruption will "sink into" incorruption and mortality will "sink into" immortality.

Paul had put on the new man. He had worn Christ to the point that he could not wait to sink into God's habitation. God's promises are given to us as garments that we are learning to wear. They don't always work as we think they should in this world but are completely received in heaven. When we step into His promises, in the presence behind the veil, we are stepping into new life.

So in the end, we will sink out of our limitations and sink fully into the eternal habitation prepared for us.

The life we live is a divine dressing room of God and we are putting on our wedding garments:

Now I saw a new heaven and a new earth, for the first heaven and the first earth had passed away. Also there was no more sea. Then I, John, saw the holy city, New Jerusalem, coming down out of heaven from God, prepared as a bride adorned for her husband. (Revelation 21:1–2)

Core Scriptures:
2 Corinthians 5:1–8; Romans 14:17; Colossians 3:10; Hebrews 6:19–20;
10:19–23

81

GOD IS BUILDING A CITY

One day, the city of Jerusalem will touch down on the new earth as a beautiful city. John describes his experience with the angel in Revelation:

Then one of the seven angels who had the seven bowls filled with the seven last plaques came to me and talked with me, saying, "Come, I will show you the bride, the Lamb's wife" and he carried me away in the Spirit to a great and high mountain, and showed me the great city, the holy Jerusalem, descending out of heaven from God, having the glory of God. Her light was like a most precious stone, like a japer stone, clear as crystal. (Revelation 21:9–11)

Imagine we are the bride, the Lamb's wife, and that we form a city fourteen hundred miles wide, fourteen hundred miles long and fourteen hundred miles high. The Lamb's wife is a living city and we are the living stones compacted together, God's habitation in the Spirit.

John goes on to say: "But I saw no temple in it, for the Lord God Almighty and the Lamb are its Temple. The city had no need of the sun or of the moon to shine in it, for the glory of God illuminated it. The Lamb is its light" (Revelation 21:22–23).

God spoke to Abraham, asking him to leave his country and sojourn in the land of promise. By faith, Abraham dwelt in the land of promise, a foreign land because he was waiting for the city whose builder and maker is God.

The promises God makes are actually His habitation on the earth and our habitation in eternity. His every word spoken to you becomes a habitation or dwelling place for God in the Spirit.

In the course of time, our capacity to believe increases and we enter into the fullness of the Spirit, which is shared in promise. It doesn't happen overnight, because we must move from our natural man into a spiritual man whose mind is set on the Spirit.

God wasn't trying to give Joseph a great ministry where he influenced the Pharaoh and led nations into prosperity through adversity. He was moving promise into promise into promise. He was building the city of God. No, not Cairo or Jerusalem. He was building the holy Jerusalem that is in heaven now but will soon come to earth.

Joseph was a part of the promise that God made to Abraham, which was that his descendants would be strangers in a land that was not their own. Joseph was part of a string of promises that has continued to this day.

Every word of God is more than its immediate meaning and the inhabiting of His word is building a place for God to dwell. When the New Jerusalem comes, we will have become a dwelling place for God. That is why there is no temple in the New Jerusalem, because God is the temple.

The promises of God, His word to me, are God's dwelling place within me through my watching over His word in hopeful anticipation. I am no longer anxious about the word being fulfilled on earth because the word has become more than the promise it carries. It is my dwelling place for God in the Spirit.

Every promise given, every word spoken, is the impartation of the divine nature of God. When held fast and firm, it becomes our eternal dwelling place.

Core Scriptures:
Revelation 21:9–23; Hebrews 11:8–10; Ephesians 2:21–2; John 14:2, 23;
Hebrews 10:23; 2 Peter 1:2–4

82

I GO TO PREPARE A PLACE FOR YOU

Jesus said, "Let not your heart be troubled; you believe in God, believe also in Me. In My Father's house are many mansions; if it were not so, I would have told you. I go to prepare a place for you. And if I go and prepare a place for you, I will come again and receive you to Myself; that where I am, there you may be also. And where I go you know and the way you know." (John 14:1–4)

Where are these mansions? Where is the Father's house? Where is the place Jesus went to prepare for us? And how does He come again and receive us to Himself so that where He is, we may also be?

No wonder Thomas was confused, saying to Jesus,

"Lord, we do not know where You are going, and how can we know the way?"

Jesus said to him, "I am the way, the truth, and the life. No one comes to the Father except through Me." (John 14:5–6)

For years, I thought these passages referred to the new birth, heavenly mansions and the second coming of Jesus. And, for sure, they do, culminating with New Jerusalem coming down from heaven. But right now, the city is being built and its mansions are being occupied. We are invited to occupy them now, the place that Jesus has prepared for us.

This took me a while to grasp.

First, I had to see that my dwelling place can either be in the Spirit or the flesh. I can walk in the flesh and see corruption, or I can walk in the Spirit and see everlasting life. Simply, my place of personal dwelling, living in the Spirit and not the flesh, will bring me the fruit of the Spirit—love, joy, peace, longsuffering, goodness, kindness, faithfulness, gentleness, and self-control. This is the fruit of the Spirit, the very essence of the nature of God. This is the divine nature of God.

But besides sowing to the Spirit or to the flesh, setting our mind on the Spirit or the flesh or even walking in the Spirit and not the flesh, the image that helped me the most was seeing John the Beloved on the island of Patmos.

John says, "I was in the Spirit on the Lord's Day and I heard behind me a loud voice as of a trumpet." (Revelation 1:10) John was "in the Spirit" and he heard a voice behind him that sounded like a trumpet:

> "I am the Alpha and the Omega, the First and the Last," and "what you see write in a book and send it to the seven churches which are in Asia..."

> Then I turned to see the voice that spoke with me. And having turned I saw seven golden lampstands, and in the mist of the seven lampstands One like the Son of Man, clothed with a garment down to the feet and girded about the chest with a golden band. His head and hair were white like wool, as white as snow,

and His eyes like a flame of fire; His feet were like fine brass, as if refined in a furnace, and His voice as the sound of many waters. (Revelation 1:11-15)

John, a prisoner on the island of Patmos, in the Spirit on the Lord's Day, heard a voice behind him and turned to see the glorified Christ, Jesus, the Son of Man. Then, Jesus took Him on a journey that we are still interpreting to this day.

After the messages to the seven churches were given to John, (recorded in chapters two and three of Revelation), the trumpet sounded again.

> After these things, I looked, and behold, a door standing open in heaven. And the first voice which I heard was like a trumpet speaking to me, saying, "Come up here, and I will show you things which must take place after this."

> Immediately I was in the Spirit; and behold, a throne set in heaven and One sat on the throne." (Revelation 4:1–2)

This just gets so wild.

Now, John is in heaven in the throne room looking into the future. Then, in his third encounter, in chapter twenty-one, John is carried away in the Spirit to a great and high mountain to see the great city, the holy Jerusalem, descending out of heaven from God.

> And he carried me away in the Spirit to a great and high mountain, and showed me the great city, the Holy Jerusalem descending out of heaven from God, having the glory of God. (Revelations 21:10-11a)

John was going to places Jesus had prepared for him, all while he was a prisoner on the island of Patmos.

Core Scriptures:
John 14:1–6; Galatians 6:8; Revelation 1:10–15; Revelation 4:1–2;
Revelation 21:9–11

83

IN THE PRESENCE OF HIM

John was in the Spirit and saw the glorified Christ, the Son of Man. He went to heaven and found himself in the throne room. After looking into the future, he found himself carried away in the Spirit to a great and high mountain to be shown the great city, the holy Jerusalem, descending out of heaven in God's glory.

Wow. This is some place that Jesus has prepared for us!

When I began to understand this, I began to live more purposefully in the Spirit. I found that God's promises were to be believed in the Spirit. Abraham understood that and, like John, also saw in the Spirit.

> (as it is written, "I have made you a father of many nations,") in the presence of Him whom he believed—God, who gives life to the dead and calls those things which do not exist as though they did; who, contrary to hope, in hope believed, so that he became the father of many nations, according to what was spoken, "so shall your descendants be." (Romans 4:17-18)

Abraham was in the Spirit, in His presence, and he believed. In His presence, Abraham hoped contrary to hope (natural hope), and through his hope, he believed. As a reward for his faith, Abraham became the father of many nations. He did all this in His presence. God's promises are meant to be believed in His presence, in the place that Jesus has prepared for us.

Let's look at this another way.

Hebrews 6:18b–20 explains Abraham's faith and patience:

> We might have strong consolation, who, having fled for refuge to lay hold of the hope set before us. This hope we have as an anchor of the soul, both sure and steadfast, and which enters the presence behind the veil, where the forerunner has entered for us, even Jesus, having become high priest forever according to the order of Melchizedek.

So Jesus went to prepare a place for us; and now, in the hope set before us, we enter into the Presence behind the veil. Jesus is the most hopeful man I know. His very presence exudes hope. He cannot look at us and see despair because He sees His work finished and our needs met.

He cannot deny Himself, so He urges us to believe, to hope contrary to hope and through that hope to believe. In the Spirit, in His promises, I am experiencing eternity. I am healed in His presence now. Here, I am forgiven and loved in His presence.

In fact, there is nothing that has been spoken that has not already been accomplished in the presence behind the veil. That is why God calls things in His presence that do not exist here (in our current world) as though they do, because they do. They do exist. They are finished and are our point of fellowship.

You are not crazy. You believed and you pleased your Father. The circumstances can be anything other than what you expect. It doesn't matter, because He spoke. But the purpose of the promise is to impart His divine nature. You must spend time in the promise in the presence behind the veil, celebrating and holding fast to your confidence and hope. The presence behind the veil is the womb of God, where our promises mature in His faithfulness.

Christ's death, burial and resurrection have prepared us to come to the Father, and through His promises, nods, words and His every communication through His Holy Spirit, He has made a place for us to dwell behind the veil.

Core Scriptures:
Revelation 4, 5; John 8:56; Romans 4:17–25; Hebrews 6:18–20; Romans 15:13; Hebrews 10:19–23

84

EXPANDING OUR CAPACITY IN CHRIST

Christ has prepared a place for us. We are learning to live in that place now.

In our Father's house are many mansions and, as we keep His word, the Father and Son come in love and make us their home through the Holy Spirit. The Greek word for "mansion" and "home" is the same. The more we keep His word, receive His precious promises, believe them and enter into the hope they inspire, the greater will be our capacity to become God's dwelling place.

This is what David meant when he prayed,

> I will run the course of Your commandments, for You shall enlarge my heart. (Psalm 119:32)

In other words, David was praying, "Increase my capacity to hold your word in my heart so I can run inside of these wonderful commandments and live." The more we see and keep, the more we avail ourselves to become a home for Father and Jesus in love.

The New Jerusalem will be made of living stones, those who have become His habitation in the Spirit. That is why there is no temple in the New Jerusalem because the Lord God Almighty and the Lamb are its temple. The city has no need of sun or moon to shine in it for the glory of God illuminates it. The Lamb is its light and we have become the dwelling place for God in the Spirit.

When John saw this, he wrote,

> Then I, John, saw the holy city, New Jerusalem, coming down out of heaven from God, prepared as a bride adorned for her husband. And I heard a loud voice from heaven saying, "Behold the tabernacle of God is with men, and He will dwell with them, and they shall   be His people. God Himself will be with them and be their God." (Revelation 21:2–3)

The New Jerusalem is built of living stones, small and large, "in whom the whole building, being fitted together, grows into a holy temple in the Lord, in whom you also are being built together for a dwelling place of God in the Spirit." (Ephesians 2:21–22)

What is so wonderful is that we are all given opportunities to increase and enlarge our capacity for God.

Yes. It is arduous and sometimes treacherous to believe God in the midst of such warring in this world, but that, too, is part of the process of exchanging the natural life for the spiritual life. It is our valuing, practicing, beholding, enduring, loving, and longing for His presence and His word that expand our hearts, allowing us to become His home. The trials will come to displace the word from our hearts but, after every trial, God promises that there will be a new baptism of His love poured into our hearts by the Holy Spirit.

God's word, held and observed by His Spirit, brings us experiences in Christ that allow us to hear more, see more, understand more, turn more to Him and be healed. We literally become the promise we behold. Christ is the word made flesh and dwells among us and in us. He is the hope of glory.

We will be sluggish at times, discouraged, despondent, betrayed and tempted to sell our birthright for immediate relief. But God, who has planted His seed in us, will call us forward. Out of ashes, we arise and see our folly. We will cry out to Him and receive our forgiveness.

Our inheritance is in Christ and cannot be lost or stolen in Him. Into our inheritance, we run, running into Christ and His finished work. Seated with Christ, we will see that the work has been finished from the foundation of the world and that we have been given the privilege of entering into this finished work one revelation at a time, one promise at a time and one exchange at a time.

Core Scriptures:
John 14:1–6, 23; Psalm 119:32; Revelation 21:22–23; 21:2–3; Ephesians 2:21–22; I Peter 2:4-5; Romans 5:1-5

85

REIGNING WITH CHRIST

Seated in heavenly places in Christ, we reign with Him on the earth as a kingdom of priests to our God. This dual destiny of heavenly citizenship and earthly reign is our inheritance, for we are receiving a kingdom that cannot be shaken in the midst of everything that can be shaken and is being shaken.

Some kind of fun!

Seated with Christ on His throne, we are aware that the nations are raging and people are plotting for their own vanity. Their kings and rulers are taking counsel together to break off Christ's rule. Believing they can rid themselves of what has already been accomplished and finished, they rise with impatience, intimidation, and hatred of Christ.

We, who sit in the heavens, shall laugh. We laugh in Christ, in His completed work, just as we have learned to laugh at all our own strivings and failings. The Lord holds all in derision as He declares more certainly, every passing day, His choosing of us in Christ—many sons and daughters brought into glory.

The word goes forth:

> Ask of Me and I will give You the nations as Your inheritance, and the ends of the earth as Your possession. You shall break them with a rod of iron; You shall dash them to pieces like a potter's vessel. (Psalm 2:8–9)

In His presence behind the veil, we have learned to sit with Christ, to live in His promises, feed on His faithfulness and rejoice completely in the hope that will be revealed. We live in two worlds, reigning from heaven and reigning on earth—yet, soon, it will be one world.

For now, the place of greatest authority is in the presence behind the veil, where Christ our forerunner has gone before us. Here we hold fast to the confession of our hope without wavering. He is faithful and will also bring His promises to fruition.

No, we are not moved from our seat in Christ through the wrangling of man and this temporal affliction. We are occupying the place Jesus has prepared for us.

The closing of this age draws near as the day dawns and the morning star rises in our hearts. Soon, we will be the church in glory, the sons of God revealed in the earth, delivering creation from the bondage of corruption and into the glorious liberty of the children of God. Christ will be revealed in His church before coming for it as He brings many sons to glory. Our faith, tested and tried, will praise and glorify the revelation of Jesus Christ when He comes to be glorified in His saints.

So we enter daily into the presence behind the veil. We behold completely what the Lord has finished; enjoying by faith what has not yet become sight, as though it has. Glorifying God, we grow stronger and stronger in faith, fully convinced that what He has promised in His presence, He is able to perform.

Then the culmination of the ages as the bride, the Lamb's wife, comes down from a new heaven into a new earth, a city compacted, His living stones. We who have kept His word have become the habitation of God in the Spirit. The Father wipes away every tear from our faces as death is swallowed up in victory. His tender touch validates all loss and sacrifice, all leaving and forgiving, as His victory swallows up death.

I have seen this in the scriptures and experienced this in small moments behind the veil in His presence. I have danced and laughed. I have sung and rejoiced in His presence. I have entered into these promises and found them living and breathing with the life of God and they have become my life.

I have lost my life, laid it down at the foot of the cross. I wish I could say that I laid it down nobly, but in actuality, it has been pretty pathetic. Still, it doesn't matter though, for Christ is my life and when He is revealed, I will be revealed with Him in glory. So will you.

Through the Son of God, who gave His life for you, through the promises of God, He has given to you, and through the pilgrimage of time, something wonderful and amazing has happened. You have become one in Christ.

Our struggles of faith and our struggles to understand God form the divine dressing room for our wedding attire. We have constructed a building with gold, silver and precious stones on the foundation of Christ. This is our dwelling place in the Spirit—costly on earth, priceless in heaven.

Today, we sit with Him, laugh with Him, and rejoice in His finished work. We enter into His presence, bringing Him our confession of hope while acknowledging His faithfulness. Today, we endure so we can reign with Him. Holding fast to our confession, we can hold fast to our place in Him.

It is glorious here in His presence. Heaven is ablaze in praise and thanksgiving to the Lamb. Joy is unspeakable and, at times, inexpressible and available to us all now. The glassy sea mixed with fire is our dance floor as we rehearse the Song of Moses and the Song of the Lamb. He has overcome!

We choose to be here rather than fret in the storms of life. We are not escaping. We are occupying until He comes. We are being translated into His likeness from glory to glory as we behold His glory in the face of Jesus. Jesus went and prepared a seat for each one of us in His presence. Our seat is vacant until we occupy it in the Lord.

Had I known what I know now, I would have entered sooner. I would have lived unchallenged, knowing I cannot be challenged in Christ. I would have been fearless, yet trusting, in the face of adversity. I would have rested in His love, fed on His faithfulness and boasted of His goodness.

But I only know what I know because of my journey of discovery. Finding treasure was the revelation. Setting out to buy the field was my journey to transformation, which has become the context of the promises that are mine in Christ Jesus.

Your journey is the same discovery of treasure and His pleasure. Leaving all to buy the field, you are a pilgrim on the earth.

He is not ashamed to be called your God. You are greatly loved, highly favored, and you bring much pleasure to Your Father!

Core Scriptures:
Hebrews 2:10; Ephesians 2:6; Revelation 3:21; Revelation 5:10; Psalm 2:1–9; Psalm 110:1–4; II Thessalonians 1:10: Hebrews 6:18–20; Psalm 37:3; John 14:1–4; 2 Peter 1:16–19; Romans 4:17-21; 8:18–21; Revelation 21:1–8; 2 Peter 1:2–4; 1 Corinthians 3:11–13; Revelation 15:1–5; 2 Corinthians 3:18; 2 Corinthians 4:6; Hebrews 11:13–16

Made in the USA
Charleston, SC
15 March 2013